What Ministers Wish
Church Members
Knew

What Ministers Wish Church Members Knew

Jan G. Linn

St. Louis, Missouri

Scripture quotations not otherwise designated are from the *New Revised Standard Version Bible*, copyright 1989, Division of Christian Education of the National Council of the Churches of Christ in the United States of America and are used by permission.

Cover illustration: Doug Hall

Art Director: Michael Dominguez

Library of Congress Cataloging–in–Publication Data

Linn, Jan.
    What ministers wish church members knew/ by Jan Linn.
    ISBN 0-8272-4230-1
    1. Church membership—United States. I. Title.
BV820.L56 1993   250   92-32944

Printed in the United States of America

For
Laverne Barnett

Acknowledgments

Writing this book has been a joyful experience. One of the reasons is the fact that I have had the opportunity to share the material with groups during its writing. Their reactions and comments have played no small role in the final shape of the book. I am, therefore, very indebted to the many ministers and lay people who have been gracious enough to invite me to talk about what I believe ministers wish their church members knew, and patient enough to listen as I have spoken. In particular, I must acknowledge the hospitality and support of the ministers and spouses and church members of the Christian Churches (Disciples of Christ) in Mississippi, and especially Bill and Sue McKnight, whom I am delighted to be able to call friends.

Congregations and groups in several other regions of the country will recognize this material from our discussions about how to revitalize the church. On a number of occasions I have used parts of the book with elders and deacons and other church leaders in attempting to help them understand the central role they play in their congregations' lives and ministries. In every instance I have come away encouraged about the people of God in today's church.

That is especially the case for the people with whom it was my joy to serve at Independence Boulevard Christian Church in Kansas City just prior to my returning to academic life. Daily I am reminded of the richness of our ministry together as it continues to inform the content of what I share in the classroom. I know I am a better minister and teacher than I would be for having had the opportunity to serve in that congregation.

As important as that ministry was in my life, moving to Lexington Theological Seminary has been a marvelous blessing. This is a community of scholars that encourages and values writing for the church. My colleagues here are some of the finest people I know in the world. No one deserves to work in such a pleasant and creative environment. It comes as a gift of which one does not have to be worthy, but for which one ought to be grateful. I am.

Special thanks must go to first-year student, Nancy Geise, for typing the final draft into my personal computer to facilitate getting the appropriate disk to the publisher. I also want to say a special word of appreciation for the help and support I have received from the editor of Chalice Press, David Polk. His initial interest and unflagging enthusiasm for the book have been a source of timely encouragement.

And now one final word of appreciation. I cannot express how grateful I am to have worked on this book with my secretary, Laverne Barnett. More than typing several drafts of the material, and more than being patient beyond what anyone had a right to expect, in her quiet and gentle way she would say just enough at just the right moment to make me believe that what I was writing was worth the effort. As the project reached it completion, Laverne decided to take early retirement. If I did not know better, I would worry that her work on the book led to this decision! I do know better, though, and so I can only hope that her health will be better to her in the years ahead than it has been. If anyone deserves a good life in retirement, it is Laverne. Because of all she has done for us at the seminary, and for all she has done for the life of the church through the faculty and students with whom she has worked for more than twenty years, this book is dedicated to her.

Contents

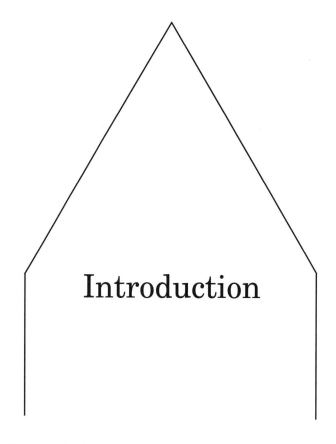

Introduction

I was asked to speak at a breakfast for ministers and mates in one of the regions of my denomination. Actually, I was a last minute substitute, so I knew they were not expecting much. I had prepared a lecture on what I thought would be a suitable topic for the occasion. The evening before I decided to forgo the lecture. I just wasn't very interested in giving it. I figured they would be even less interested in hearing it.

My mind was on other "things." For several months I had been thinking about and occasionally writing down what I believed ministers, at least the ones I knew, wished their church members knew—about ministry and about the church. I wasn't thinking about complicated theological concepts. Rather, I was thinking about things that made sense the minute you heard them; things that upon reflection one could easily recognize as important practical realities about ministry; things that often hinder the church being the church when they are ignored.

I decided to share a beginning list of things I believed ministers wished their church members knew with the ministers and their spouses, with a brief comment on them as I went along. This was not the sort of thing I ever did. But, as I said, I was a substitute speaker. How bad could it be? I did not know a single person who would be there. I knew I was leaving the next day. Why not do it? So with tongue firmly planted in cheek, I did.

To my utter amazement, they loved it! It was one of those serendipitous moments when you receive something totally unexpected and better than anything you were anticipating. What I said obviously touched a nerve in them. It was as if I had articulated what they had been thinking and feeling for a long time. Similar occasions since that time have produced the same response, confirming in me the conviction that there are some things most ministers wish their church members knew about church, ministry, and even themselves.

In the latter years of my congregational ministry, I often had moments when I wished I could sit down in a spirit of openness and candor and talk with my church members about what I believed they needed to know. I believed knowing these things could make a real difference in our church's life and witness. Not that I did not need to know them. Not that I did not need to listen to them. It was, instead, a matter of seemingly never having a time or place or setting when I could talk with them about things I wished all of us knew. I shared bits and pieces of these thoughts from time to time, but I never found the appropriate occasion when I could discuss them fully.

The response of the ministers and spouses at the breakfast made me realize that they would like to have similar conversations with their church members. I am sure there are many things church members wish their ministers knew. But we are at a time in the life of the church when respect for ministerial authority is at a low point. In some respects it is for good reason. Some ministers do not inspire confidence. A few are downright incompetent. Yet I have met more than a few ministers who have much wisdom to share with members about ministry and church life. It is a simple kind of wisdom about everyday church life. It might even be described as a commonsense wisdom that needs to be heard in the church.

Perhaps the most interesting thing about my experience of lecturing on what ministers wish their church members knew has been the response of the laity. Most of the groups to whom I have spoken have had more laity than ministers in attendance. The laity have been gracious and even enthusiastic about what they have heard. In several instances I have been asked to return to speak to a larger audience of laity. This suggests that these thoughts have more value than what might be called "ministerial commiseration." It is quite possible, if not likely, that many church members already know what their ministers want them to know, and are ready and willing to discuss it with them. They share the concern ministers have about the state of the church today. Hesitant themselves, the laity of our churches may in fact be anxiously waiting for their minister—or someone—to take the initiative to begin the discussion.

This is what I have tried to do in these pages—initiate discussion. There is no intention here to attempt to give the last word on the issues being addressed. If anything, I am seeking—as an outside observer, in a manner of speaking—only to raise them in congregations in the hope that they might become a point of ongoing discussion between minister and church members. If this kind of discussion should take place, then the book will have produced the desired goal that motivated its writing in the first place.

It may be that various groups in a church will find it beneficial to read and discuss the book. I believe the larger the circle of discussion, the greater the chance that candid dialogue between ministers and church members will strengthen the life and witness of the church. Who knows? Such discussion might even prove to be fun! Can you imagine that? At the very least, this book might help all of us—church members and ministers alike—not to take ourselves too seriously. While issues can be serious, we need a bit of a "reality check" from time to time to remind ourselves that we are not the beginning or the end of all things, even in the church—indeed, especially in the church. We are here to be responsible and to be joyful. I am convinced we can be both. So I hope readers will have fun with *What Ministers Wish Church Members Knew*. I also hope the book will contribute to the kind of open and candid dialogue on important issues between ministers and church members that can only strengthen the life and witness of their churches.

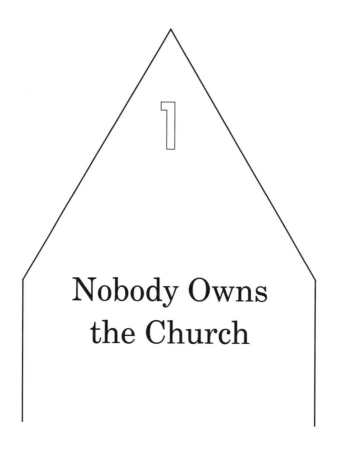

Nobody Owns
the Church

"Well, if it's not God's church, then whose is it?" So asked one of my colleagues during a faculty discussion we were having on the renewal of the church. At issue was the role of church members. We were sure we had one. We were equally sure that whatever our role was, we get into trouble if we forget that the church doesn't belong to us. We may support it, but we don't own it!

Nobody owns the church. That is about as basic as things get. The story of Pentecost makes it clear that the church is an act of God. It is not the result of human initiative or endeavor. The church was born of the Spirit. It seems such a simple thing for any church member to understand. Maybe we do understand it. We just don't want to accept it. Whichever it is, this thing of who owns the church continues to be a problem.

Soon after beginning my last pastorate, I introduced myself to the manager of a nearby store as the pastor of Independence Boulevard Church. His reply was, "Isn't that R.A. Long's church?" Not wanting to get off on the wrong foot with someone I would probably have to do business with, I said yes. The fact was, a man named R. A. Long had put up most of the money—and it took a lot of it—to build that church building many years before. The store manager knew that. For him that meant it was R. A. Long's church. I guess for him if your money builds it then you own it.

Few church members have the resources of an R. A. Long, or a John D. Rockefeller, who built Riverside Church in New York City. There are many, however, who give money for stained-glass windows, communion tables, pulpits, pews, hymn books, carpet, organs, choir robes, or sound systems. Others give generously on a regular basis to support the church budget year after year. Still others give of their time and abilities to keep the church going.

We can be glad for this kind of tangible support of the church. No congregation can thrive or survive without it. Why is it, though, that we can't keep it straight in our thinking that support of the church does not entitle one to ownership? The church does not have stockholders. It does not even have presidents or managers, although we use terms like that now. The church has servants. Nothing more and nothing less. It is a privilege that too often turns into ownership for people the church needs to remain servants.

In one church I know a Sunday school class spent several thousand dollars remodeling its room. One of their members died and left the class some additional money. They voted to use it to put an awning at the outside entrance near their classroom with their class name on it. The pastor objected on the grounds that no class should put its name on a permanent part of the outside of the building. It would give the impression that they owned that part of the church. If other classes wanted to do the same thing, the building would have a multitude of names on it, as if each class had staked out a claim on the church.

Most of the members of the class understood their pastor's concern. There were few, however, who were determined to proceed. It was the class's money, they said, and the class could do anything they wanted with it. What saved the day—or at least kept a minor conflict from becoming major—was when one of the older members of the class remembered that the church board had voted years ago not to allow names on the outside of the building.

This incident is indicative of the possessiveness some church members have about the church. When they speak of "their" church, they mean it. It is a rare thing for someone to give the church money or time with no strings attached. Somewhere along the way the basic claim of the gospel that the church belongs to God has been lost on us. The result is that we think it is our church. We run it. We decide what is done and when and by whom. We hold the power. Attend the board or session or vestry meeting of just about any church and you will see this attitude in action.

I sometimes wonder what would happen if churches suddenly got the message—the church belongs to God, and God has made Jesus lord of it! I mean really got it. I think there would be a revolution in church life overnight. I think all of us would feel a new sense of freedom in faith. Joy would characterize our life together. We would celebrate life in the knowledge that it does not belong to us, that life and church and everything is a gift from God. I suspect we would focus more on faithfulness because we would have given up the illusion of ownership. What a great day that would be.

If we understood the nature of the church, I am sure we would be more anxious to do what God wants. The apostle Paul wrote that we should lead lives that are "holy and acceptable to God, which is your spiritual worship" (Romans 12:1). I am not a Greek scholar, but in my opinion this is an inadequate translation of this verse. It really says that we should lead lives that are "holy and well-pleasing, which is our reasonable service." That, I think, gets to the heart of the matter. Because we are members of God's church, we ought to lead lives that are holy (whole) and well-pleasing to God.

That is a reasonable offering to make. It is not asking too much of us since it's God's church. Just to be acceptable is not enough. That is only to get by in the church. We may do that as long as we think the church belongs to us. But it is an altogether different matter if God owns the church. We are the guests who want to please the host. That puts things in their right place because it puts God in the right place.

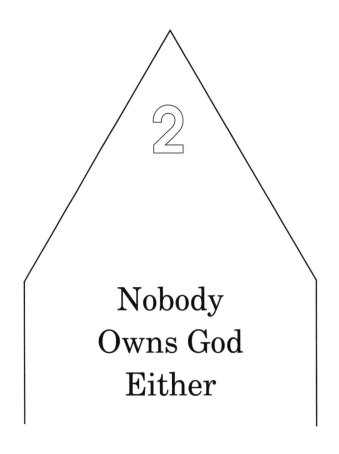

Nobody Owns God Either

Not only does nobody own the church; nobody owns God either. Some people apparently think they do, though, perhaps without even realizing it. I often hear people begin a statement about God by saying, "Well, my God...." That kind of talk bothers me. I think it suggests an ownership of God. When God becomes my God, then God is no longer God, but what I decide God is. No doubt some people want to convey the personal dimension of their relationship to God by saying "my God." In this instance, though, I think using the possessive pronoun *my* over-steps appropriate reverence for God, and reveals at least an unconscious attitude that God belongs to me.

Years ago Bible scholar and translator, J. B. Phillips, wrote a popular book entitled *Your God Is Too Small*. It was written for church members who he said were letting "inadequate conceptions of God...prevent them from catching a glimpse of the true God."[1] It was a helpful book at the time. Today, though, I think we need to go further and say that no conception of God is ever adequate! Another way to say this is: God is and always will be bigger than what any of us ever thinks. Nothing the human mind can come up with will ever fully capture God's nature or God's ways. That is why nobody owns God. God is always larger than any human thoughts about God.

I think scripture underscores the fact that much that has to do with God falls under the category of mystery. We spend so much time trying to understand God that we run the risk of forgetting that we will never fully understand God, and that is why we walk by faith and not by sight (2 Corinthians 5:7). The older I get the more life seems to be shrouded in mystery and the less I seem to be able to understand it intellectually. On top of that, it does not bother me that this is the case. When I was young I had a million questions I wanted answered. Today most of the questions do not even interest me.

Not that thinking about God is unimportant. I get paid to think about God. It is a matter of perspective. We humans tend to take ourselves too seriously. We get wrapped up in things of concern to us and lose sight of the "big" picture. We matter, but we are not all that matters. I think church members tend to forget this as much as anyone. We can get so caught up in the life we have found in Jesus Christ that we begin to think the salvation of the world depends on what we think and do. Before we know it we have become religious zealots who will stop at nothing to get people to think and believe the way we do.

We had a seminary student who would often say that he thought the problem in the church was the failure of ministers to stand for something. It was his opinion that too many ministers were afraid of offending someone if they took a stand on something they believed in. I could sympathize with this student. In some respects he was emphasizing the need for ministers to have the courage of their convictions as they lead the church. That is something worth remembering.

On the other hand, I thought that he was not as aware as he needed to be that no matter how firmly convinced he was of something, he could never hold a corner on truth. I wanted to tell him a story I heard years ago about a witness in a trial who was sworn in with the traditional oath, "Do you swear to tell the truth, the whole truth, and nothing but the truth, so help you God?" The man replied, "Sir, if I told the truth, the whole truth, and nothing but the truth, I would *be* God!"

So would any of us. We cannot know the whole truth. The best we can hope for in this life is to tell all the truth we know. I think church members of every stripe—liberal, conservative, and those in-between—would do well to keep in mind the fact that God will always be bigger than we think. If we did I do not think we would have all the fights and splits that continue to damage our witness in the world. We can know some things about God. We cannot know everything, though. Besides, what really matters is not what we know about God. Isn't it whether or not we really know God?

In the long run I believe the church would be better off if more of its members believed that nobody owns the church *and* that nobody owns God. Then we would be able to concentrate on the thing that is true—we belong to God. That is the good news. God does not belong to us, but we belong to God. That should be enough!

[1]J.B. Phillips, *Your God Is Too Small* (MacMillian Co., 1961), p. 8.

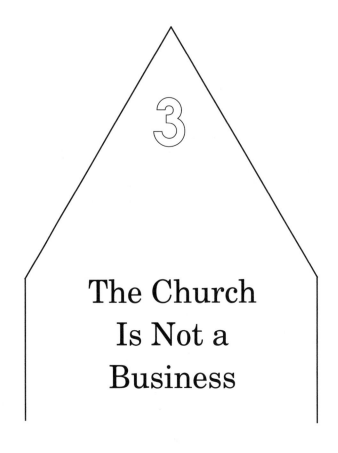

The Church
Is Not a
Business

Churches hold a 501-C tax-exempt status with the Internal Revenue Service. That means they are categorized as not-for-profit organizations. The question is, "Are they?" The churches I served were! In terms of income and expenses, at best we broke even at the end of the year. Sometimes we went in the red. But we kept going.

Churches like the ones I served live from hand to mouth. They would prefer not to, but they do. They sometimes have a few members who complain about living on the financial edge. They push to have money put aside for a "rainy" day. In one church I served I found out after I left that a few prominent members had done just that— put away several hundred thousand dollars for that "rainy" day. It began with a generous estate gift the general membership did not know about. The "rainy" day never came, so the interest kept piling up. When the others found out about the secret fund, they were less than pleased.

The men who watched over the money did not understand why the rest of the members were so upset. After all, they were looking out for the best interests of the church. And they were. That was not the problem. The problem was that they did not understand the church is not a business. It does not live in fear of a "rainy" day, and when it starts to it ceases to be the church and becomes a business.

The church is not a business for one simple reason— money is not its most important concern! It is not even its primary concern. The church's primary focus is ministry, but that is far different from making money a primary concern. Indeed, when money becomes the major concern in a church, that church has become corrupted. The reason is that it then begins to do ministry by budget, rather than doing budget by ministry. Instead of focusing on the ministry that God is calling them to do, church members focus on how much money they have and then decide what ministry they can do.

Doing ministry this way flies in the face of "walk[ing] by faith, not by sight" (2 Corinthians 5:7). This kind of church becomes a group of people who are doing only what they think they can do. They may not realize it, but God never gets in the picture. These are the churches whose members are tempted to think the church belongs to them. They limit ministry to what they think they can afford, except when it comes to themselves. Then they can often afford more than they thought they could.

For a business the infamous "bottom line" is profit and loss. Everything else is secondary. In the church the "bottom line" is people. Everything else is secondary to that, including money. Businesses have to be concerned with money. Churches do not. Churches can think in a different way. Nothing is an end in itself in the church. All resources serve to support doing ministry.

The church is not a business because it does not have a product to market. The gospel is not a product to be sold. Attraction rather than promotion would be a healthier way for church members to think of evangelism. The gospel is a life to be lived. Winning friends and influencing people is not a standard the church should ever accept for its idea of success. Success in the church is faithfulness to the demands of the gospel. Nothing more and nothing less constitutes success. Churches with lots of money and churches with no money can be successful. Churches whose size gives them power and churches whose size gives them no power can be successful. It all hinges on their commitment to live the gospel. The most winsome force for the church is not a sales pitch, but the attractiveness of its commitment to live as the body of Christ.

The emphasis in recent years has been to think of the task of ordained ministry in "management" terms. I have a colleague who uses management terms, but he does not think about the ministry that way. Unfortunately many people do. It is a dangerous way of thinking about ministry and the church. God save us from ministers who think the church is something to be managed and from lay people who support them in doing it. Ministry is not a matter of managing a business, and the church is not a business to be managed.

The church is a called community. Its life originates in God. It is not the result of human endeavors, nor will it be sustained solely by what we do. Its power is from beyond itself, or it is not a church. It may be a smooth-running organization. It may use the language of a church. It may look like a church. But it is not the church. This does not mean that human effort is unimportant. It is only to say that the church needs to remember that its life is not of its own making, and that when we begin to think of the church as a business, we have given in to the kind of thinking that undercuts the very reason the church exists—to do ministry.

Spread sheets can never tell the church's story. Assets and liabilities are hardly what we are about. The church is neither a profit nor a not-for-profit corporation because it is not a corporation in the first place. The state may call it that. That is the language of the culture, not the church. What is important is for church members not to let the language of the dominant culture influence the way we think about who we are. We are a called community. We are the body of Christ. The body of Christ can never be a business and remain the body of Christ.

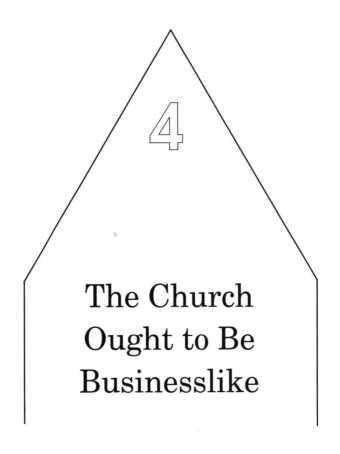

The Church Ought to Be Businesslike

As long as we do not think of the church as a business, we are free to do some things in the church in a business-like way. One is to pay all the bills. Churches that do not pay their bills ought to stop calling themselves a church. They are a poor witness to the gospel. We may be citizens of another kingdom, but as long as we live in Caesar's realm, we ought to pay Caesar what we owe. Heavenly work does not excuse us from earthly obligations.

One "bill" that more than a few churches are negligent about is paying guest speakers a reasonable honorarium, and to pay them in a timely fashion. Many times a person will spend time preparing a sermon or a series of lectures, spend money in travel, only to be told after the event that the check will be sent. It is shameful how many times that check is sent months later, sometimes not at all, and often in an amount that barely covers expenses. No one should have to ask a church to pay them for services rendered. They don't do this sort of thing for the money. Most honorariums would not make it worthwhile. They do expect to be paid, however, and especially to be reimbursed for expenses.

One Easter I was asked to speak at a sunrise service in a community about an hour from my home. I arose at 4:30 a.m. and drove to the service, preached, attended a breakfast, then returned home. Two months later I received a check in the mail for $25. I started to send it back. This is not the way a church, or a community of churches, should do ministry. To my mind it is shameful.

A church I know asked me if I would help them find a supply preacher. When they told me how much—how little actually—they wanted to pay, I told them it would be difficult to find someone. After a board discussion, they decided to keep the amount of the honorarium as it was, since, as they said to me, "these people already have another job." What this church was saying was that it wanted someone else to pay its way. It could use a little sense of business responsibility.

Not only should churches pay a just amount for services rendered, and pay it on time, they should also keep all finances aboveboard. We should never be afraid of an audit of the books, for example, especially a "management" audit to review financial procedures. The church should welcome such a review. It is a way to show that we know how to be in the world but not of it. We can do things in a businesslike manner without thinking of ourselves as a business. I have had the experience of finding out after the fact that the church's books were kept worse than the way some people keep their checkbook ledger.

When my daughter had her first checking account as a college freshman, she was thrilled. She considered herself financially independent. That is, until she started getting her overdraft notices. The problem was, she found it easy to write checks, but saw no reason to record them in the ledger. It got so messed up the only solution was to close the account and start over.

Some churches are almost as bad. The books are kept with less than care and precision. One church I know had a treasurer maintain memorial fund money the way the government is keeping our Social Security. It was on paper but the money had been spent. It seems the treasurer decided to put the memorial money into the general account to help pay the bills. She knew exactly how much memorial money there was supposed to be. It just wasn't there when it was needed.

As a student I served a church where the treasurer took home the Sunday collection to count. He was the only one who knew what the amount was. He was an honest man, but that was not the point. If a question ever arose, how would he have accounted for the money? What was worse, he would often wait a week or two before he would make a deposit. If he had become ill or died, the church's money would have been tied up in the courts without any reliable way to know how much money belonged to the church. Yet his family and a few friends in the church resisted any effort to change this situation.

This may have been an extreme case, but it points to the importance of the church doing business in a business-like manner. How the church handles the money with which it is entrusted is a sacred responsibility. The fact that the church is not in the business of making money is no excuse for being careless or irresponsible in keeping what money it does have. Churches should set an example of competence in money matters. They should want no special favors or ask anyone's indulgence when it comes to paying their own way. Giving an account of the hope that is within us (1 Peter 3:15) is true in regard to material as well as spiritual affairs.

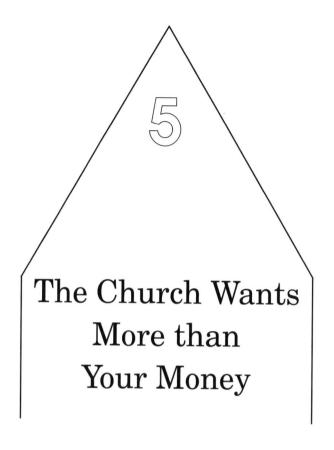

The Church Wants More than Your Money

I have lost count of the number of times I have heard people say, "All my church cares about is money." What with all the TV preachers singing the same song about how their show will go off the air unless the viewer sends in a contribution immediately, it is little wonder that people think this way. What gets me are all the "free" gift offers TV preachers talk about. Whenever I hear them I think to myself that I must be missing something. They keep saying that viewers will receive a "free" gift if they send in a generous contribution. I guess this is a different way of thinking about something being "free."

I am sure there are some churches that are almost this bad. One of my students told me that the senior minister she works for manages to throw in something about their church needing money in almost every sermon. Yet I believe the vast majority of churches and ministers want far more from people than their money. Before money there is the matter of commitment. No minister can survive the stress and discouragements of ministry without devoted members who manage to show love for the church's life and mission at critical moments. These are the people who make ministers believe in the church as the body of Christ. They give more time to the church than anyone has a right to expect, and they do it without being asked. I'll take a loyal church member before a pocketbook any day. Any minister worth her or his salt will.

I know more than a few churches that do not lack for money whenever they want to do something. That is not the problem. The problem is they don't want to do anything. Most of the members do not attend with any regularity. Most of those who do want to come and leave on Sunday and be left alone the rest of the week. These churches are dead. They have plenty of money. They just don't have any life. I don't know any ministers who want to serve in such churches.

When ministers get together to talk about the church, the number one topic of conversation is not the collection plate. It is, instead, concern over the lack of commitment to the church's life by so many church members and their unwillingness to use their talents and abilities in the ministry. Churches are hungry for members who will teach, sing in the choir, lead a mission to the homeless, take time to pray and study and attend spiritual life retreats. Last year I was asked by two different churches to lead weekend retreats on spirituality. In both cases the retreat was canceled for lack of interest. I thought perhaps the fact that I was to be the retreat leader was the problem. In both instances the ministerial leadership thought otherwise. They believed the problem was an issue of priorities, and the choice their members made was quite discouraging.

One of the first bouts student pastors have with discouragement comes when they realize getting church members to want to do anything is a constant struggle. Church members hire the student to do the ministry, and they pay the bills. That is how it works in many churches. First-year students begin to wonder if this is the way it will always be. If it is, they are not sure they want to spend the rest of their lives in ministry. We who teach them can only say that it is not this way in every church, but it is this way in a lot of churches, and they need to be realistic about the choices church members often make.

The fact is the church is an organization of volunteers. Anyone who works with volunteers knows firsthand the problem of getting them to make a reliable commitment to the work. The church is no different. Ministers are committed to the life and ministry of the church full time. All our waking hours—and not a few of our sleeping ones—are devoted to the church. But to get anything done, we are dependent on volunteers for whom the church is at best a part-time involvement.

At the same time I have been amazed at the willingness of some church members to give the time they do. Most people have more demands on their time than time to meet them. Choices have to be made. It is always easier to give money to the church than to give oneself. The ministers I know want the people before they even think about their money. Committed church members I know feel the same way. The reason is they know that giving one's attention and time is the only way a person can grow spiritually. It does not happen on its own. Being a church member does not make one a Christian, and certainly not a mature Christian. The sad truth is that churches are filled with members who remain "babes" in Christ, who have hardly moved beyond an elementary knowledge of or experience with Jesus Christ as Savior and Lord. These people are not bad. They are busy. Because they are busy, they are easy prey to the tempter's snare wherein they confuse giving money with giving themselves.

The real problem in church life today is not money. Money is always a symptom, never a disease. My denomination has seen a serious decline in its financial support the last few years. Unfortunately, our response has been to launch the largest capital campaign we have ever undertaken. The intentions behind it are good—get people involved in something that is tangible. But it fails to address the real issue, which is a growing schism between the denominational leaders and the people in the local congregations born from a perception at the local level that the denomination is out of touch with the views and needs of the people who support it. What is worse, it has the potential of making people believe that all the church is interested in is their money.

I know some of our leaders personally, and I know this is not what they believe. Perception, however, is often reality for most people. Somewhere along the way ministers and other church leaders of every stripe have made the rank and file membership believe that all they are interested in is their money. But it is not true. The church needs *us*—all of us—our attention, our devotion, our presence, our talents, our time. If it does not have these, it may as well not have our money. *We* are what the church wants most from us. Don't ever let anyone tell you otherwise.

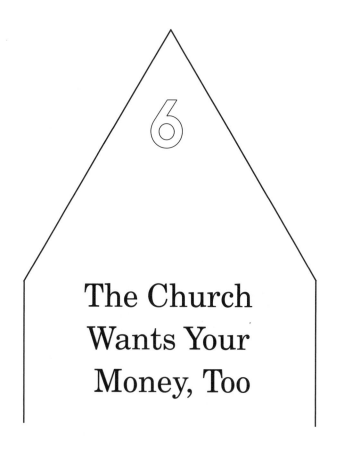

The Church
Wants Your
Money, Too

If your church has you, then it also wants and needs your money. For some reason churches have trouble admitting this openly, and many members have trouble hearing it when it is discussed. We get very possessive and defensive around money talk. Many mainline churches are at the opposite extreme from TV preachers. Those TV evangelists can't talk about anything but money; we can't talk about it at all without feeling awkward or embarrassed.

One of the most uncomfortable parts of ministry is the annual "stewardship" emphasis. We go to great lengths to call it anything and everything but what it is—asking for money! Of course, it is more than that. It is a time to educate people about the ministry of the church. In some churches it is a time when people are asked to sign up for a committee or activity for the coming year. Yet when all is said and done, if financial pledges fail to meet expectations, the minister feels like his ministry is shaky, and the treasurer goes into a "Chicken Little" state of panic, screaming, "The sky is falling, the sky is falling!"

Early in my ministry I thought asking for money was a bit "crass" for a spiritual organization such as the church. Certainly it was beneath my preaching on it. I was called to preach the gospel of Jesus Christ. Money was somebody else's responsibility. I smile at myself as I think about it now. How naive I was. Indeed, how limited—and actually unscriptural—my views were. Nothing shows where one's heart is more than where one spends one's money. Jesus said it: "Where your treasure is, there your heart will be also" (Matthew 6:21).

Sometimes we are challenged to put our money where our mouth is. Jesus challenges us to go one better. He wants us to put our money where our heart is. That is why the church wants more than our money in the first place. If it has our heart, then it will have our money, too—at least a reasonable portion of it. Church members who have given their hearts to the church know the church also needs their money. When we are devoted to something, we want to support it financially. At the same time, though, I have learned that there is no substitute for such support. More than once I have had church members say that had they known we needed money they would have tried to help a little more. Early on in ministry I would have thought that they should have given the "extra" without having to be asked. Now I know that is silly. Not only is there nothing wrong with telling people the church wants and needs their money, it usually stimulates them to give more than they otherwise would.

In my last pastorate we spent a year educating the members on the true financial state of our church. For years the church had relied on special bequests and gifts to make its budget, but that source had begun to decline. Yet the members had never been told that they needed to raise their support or the church was going to be in a financial crisis. There had been a standing tradition in the church that the church's financial condition was not to be discussed openly, lest people think we were not a strong church. We finally managed to break the silence, and the response of membership was both shock and increased giving. All we had to do was to ask.

One of the problems churches face when it comes to money is what I call "political" giving. This is when church members give when the church's program and thematic emphases suit them, and when they don't, then the members do not give. Political giving is the bane of church life. It puts pressure on the minister to lead the people where they want to go instead of where the will of God might lead them. It implies that sermons should not disturb anyone or upset the status quo.

The film *Mass Appeal*, stars Jack Lemmon as an older priest who has carved out a comfortable niche for himself in his parish by telling people whatever they want to hear, but has his world upset by a young man studying for the priesthood who will not compromise his integrity so easily. Early in the story the young man preaches a sermon that upsets the congregation. Lemmon chastises him for doing it, at one point saying, "It is no accident that the offering comes right after the sermon. It is a Nielson rating on how you've done."

That is a statement that acknowledges both the reality and the danger of political giving. The church does want and need the financial support of its people, but it can never want it so much that it compromises the integrity of the gospel in order to get it. Every minister and every member who cares about the church lives with the stress and tension that go with needing money to do God's work, but when money becomes more important than the gospel, ministry is lost.

Another frustration is that sometimes the people who fuss the most about how a church spends its money give the least to it. That has always puzzled me. One would think it would be just the opposite. That is, those who give the most would fuss the most. Yet the most generous givers I have known have done so with no strings attached, in the sense that they did not see their giving in terms of "griping rights." They were usually the last to complain about church finances. They wanted their money used wisely and responsibly, but their main concern was that the church have what it needed to do the ministry it was called to do. It was not how much these people gave to the church that mattered. It was the attitude with which they gave it. They knew how to love without possessing. I believe such people are among the beloved of God. Every church needs all of them it can get because the church always needs their money, too.

Good Ministers
Don't Cost—
They Pay

One of the most trying conflicts I ever had with a church treasurer had to do with the way he viewed the salaries of the staff. When budget time came around, he insisted on including health care, pension and social security in one salary total for each staff member. I argued that the actual salary should be listed separately from these other items. Otherwise figures would be misleading by unfairly inflating the salary packages. Fringe benefits are important, but they don't pay the mortgage. Salary is money I can take home. Besides, I knew that the company he used to work for did not list all his fringe benefits in his salary package. His response was, "Well, I want to let the church members know how much the staff costs them."

That is the way some church members think about staff—how much they cost. We become line items in a budget, and sometimes the largest item at that. That immediately makes church members wonder if the staff is earning its pay, or perhaps being paid too much. Sometimes this leads to inane methods of accountability such as reporting the number of visits the minister has made or how many counseling sessions were held. A smart church member, on the other hand, knows that a good church staff does not cost, they pay. A competent, dedicated staff will save the church more money than they will ever cost. Good ministers and clerical staff make wise use of their time. That alone saves the church money. They also work well together. That saves a church more money than it can count, and a lot more than money can buy.

One of the reasons church members think about their minister in terms of costs around budget time, regardless of her commitment or competence, is because they do not realize how much poor leadership really costs them. Poor leadership wastes time and energy. Its drain on the emotional, intellectual, and spiritual energy of a church can be severe. Good ministerial leadership does just the opposite. It contributes positively to the emotional, intellectual and spiritual health of a church. In no sense is good ministerial leadership "overhead." It is not a debit in the church account. It is a resource that should always be viewed as an asset.

A simple thing that so many church members fail to think about is that when they think of staff salaries as "overhead," the cost to morale is high. Nothing gets ministers down faster than feeling like they are regarded as a cost factor in a budget. One of the ways churches can show appreciation for ministers is precisely by not thinking of them in this way. The issue is not salary so much as it is the attitude of church members about it.

I remember many years ago a colleague who served a three-church charge sharing his excitement when the smallest of his congregations gave him a generous check for Christmas, an amount he did not think they could afford. It humbled him to know they had sacrificed just to show him how much they appreciated his ministry. It was not the money that counted. The amount was actually very small. What mattered was the attitude the money symbolized. In fact, their gesture was worth more to him than the money ever could be. That is the way it is for most of the ministers I know. They have to have money to live, but they never want to be viewed as a cost factor in a church budget.

There is a sign that appears on empty billboards from time to time that reads, "Advertising doesn't cost, it pays." There is truth in that statement. Money spent can sometimes be an investment that yields far more than it costs. I believe that good ministerial leadership—indeed, good church staff all around—is an investment that pays more than it costs. Churches that realize how true this is have taken a significant step in understanding the value of good leadership. These are the smart churches. They know how to add. They know what really costs, and they know what really pays.

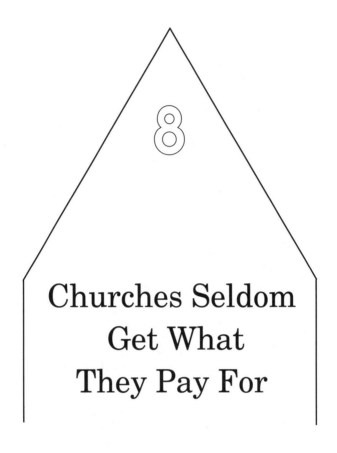

Churches Seldom Get What They Pay For

While we are talking about money, there is something else that needs to be said, which is, churches may not realize it, but most always they never get what they pay for from their minister. They get more. Most of the ministers I know are very committed Christians. They want to do their best for their people every day. They work long hours. A fifty to sixty hour work week is not uncommon for the minister of a medium-size congregation. Moreover, no holiday or vacation is ever free from the emergencies of illness or death in the church family. What minister has not been called back for a funeral or crisis in a church family?

Days off for the average minister have to be protected like a maximum security prison. The ministry is not the kind of job a person leaves at the office. Ministers are on call twenty-four hours a day, and every good minister knows it—and wouldn't have it any other way. I remember one January spending five Saturday nights in a row at a hospital emergency room with families of church members. This is the way a minister's day off usually goes. Invariably someone has surgery on your day off. A funeral is scheduled. A problem occurs at the church office that needs your immediate attention. People say that you just have to stay away from the church or say no to people. It is not that easy. How can a minister say no to an elder who is facing open-heart surgery and wants the pastor to say a prayer before they operate? How can you tell a woman who has just lost the ninety-two-year-old mother she has cared for that you will see her tomorrow? How can you tell your secretary, who has a homeless family of six children standing in her office, that you do not want to be bothered by such problems on your day off?

All of us have, of course, heard stories of ministers who spend more time on the golf course than in ministry, and nowadays it is not uncommon to hear about young ministers who try to limit ministry to eight hours a day. Unfortunately, one of our own graduates was let go by a church a couple of years ago for such foolishness, and rightly so. She learned the hard way what most students and full-time ministers already know and accept, that ministry can never be done by a time clock.

Certainly ministers cannot meet every need their church members have. Most of us need to do better at letting some things wait that can wait. Most ministers have trouble separating what is real and what is perceived when it comes to the expectations of church members. But the line between what can and cannot wait is usually pretty thin. The ministers I know want to err in doing too much than in doing too little. And most of them do it while receiving only modest salaries.

Experience tells me that church members who worry about their minister making too much money, or getting a bigger salary increase than she deserves, simply do not know the demands of time and energy ministry involves. On an hourly basis, my guess is that the average minister hardly makes minimum wage. There may be a few who are lazy, who do not earn their keep. But their numbers are few, and no one is more critical of them than their colleagues. At the same time, every year I am humbled by the tremendous sacrifice so many of our incoming students make just to come to seminary. A single-parent woman is here this year who is finishing her Ph.D. in Spanish, but who has felt the call to ministry for years and has finally decided she cannot ignore it any longer. What a financial and professional sacrifice she is making to study for ministry. She is one of those who will never give the church only what it pays for. She will always give it more. Her name is "Legion."

One might want to argue that the church is facing a leadership crisis. I could not agree more. Ministerial leadership today faces serious problems. But high pay—making more than they deserve—is not one of the problems of church leadership today. The truth is, most churches seldom get what they pay for. They get more. That is a fact of church life that never ought to be forgotten. Nobody ever goes into the ministry for the money. It is a good thing. There is none to be made. The ministry has many rewards. Money is not one of them.

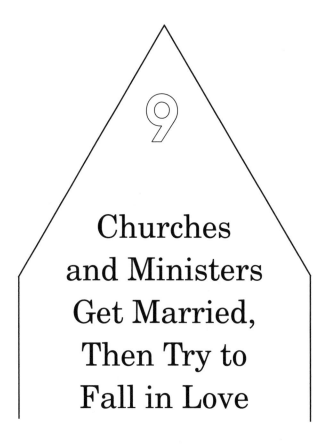

Churches and Ministers Get Married, Then Try to Fall in Love

People who get married usually fall in love first. That is why they get married, at least most of the time. I think churches and ministers do just the opposite. They get "married," then try to fall in love. A minister will begin a ministry in a church without knowing the people very well. Church members call someone to be their minister without knowing that person very well. Then they try to live together in harmony and love.

The relationship between a church and the minister is similar to a marriage in several ways. For one thing, the minister and church members do have to "live" together. They share the most personal moments of life together—marriage, divorce, birth, death, and problems of all shapes and sizes. The minister is the one person church members expect to be there when they go through such things. Sometimes the relationship is one in which the minister's presence is comfortable as well as comforting, almost like another member of the family. Other times the relationship is such that the minister's presence is awkward and makes everyone ill at ease. Then ministry becomes a "job" that has to be done. Either way, though, the minister is expected to be there, and usually is.

Ministers and churches also have to be supportive of each other, much like a married couple, if the church of which they are a part is to be healthy. There is a certain level of "companionship" between ministers and church members. Each needs to know that the other "partner" is there when needed. Each needs to feel the other's support and goodwill on a daily basis in order to cope with frustrations and disappointments. They may not always agree, but they do always need to have the best interests of the other in mind.

A bad match between a minister and a church is almost as traumatic as a bad match between a man and a woman who get married. In a bad match, the minister and the church, like a husband and wife, can pick at each other until the skin of both is irritated and even bleeding. They can tear each other down to the point where both feel bad about each other and themselves. At that point it is difficult to avoid the pain of a "divorce." And when it occurs, it is an awful experience for everyone involved. I have seen churches torn apart by the firing of a minister, even when the match was clearly a mistake.

On the other hand, a good match between a minister and church members is like a good match between a husband and wife. They love and support each other. They recognize the differences between them, and work at respecting and enjoying the uniqueness each brings to the relationship. They do not let differences of opinion color their perspective of one another. They are also realistic enough to know that conflicts are unavoidable, and sometimes even provide an opportunity for deepening the relationship when handled in a mature and constructive way.

One complicating factor in the relationship between a church and a minister is the fact that it is often "polygamous." That is, the minister marries more than one person, and if it is a multiple staff church, the members do, too. To be honest, experience shows that this fact of life puts the odds against the "marriage" making it. It is hard enough for two people to make it in a marriage. Three or more becomes a crowd, and multiplies the problems. It means the minister must learn how to be present to a lot of people at the same time, without neglecting one for another. He also has to be careful not to show favoritism, lest jealousy become a serious problem.

Church members have to avoid the same thing when there is more than one staff member. If they do not want to split the church, they must avoid playing favorites and trying to promote one staff member at the expense of another. The record of serious and destructive conflict in multiple staff churches is not one to envy. Even the staff can become "a house divided against itself." When this happens, things really are in bad shape.

It is a wonder that any "marriage" makes it these days. People from different backgrounds and needs steeped in an ethic of self-fulfillment begin what is to be a lifelong relationship. So much can and does happen that makes an already difficult situation that much harder to make work. The same is true with churches and ministers. Different people with different backgrounds, different expectations, and different personalities try to live together in a church. It is a miracle it ever works out. But it does! There are some happy "marriages"—in homes and in churches. Not without hard work. Not without numerous sacrifices. And not without, as my wedding ceremony says, "avoiding childish disputes and jealousies." It can work. When it does it is the most fulfilling experience we humans can have.

Not long ago I was invited by a recent graduate to lead a leadership workshop and to preach. The weekend was made a joyous experience just by seeing the love between the pastor and his people shared so freely. They actually had a good time with each other. They laughed together and disagreed together. They respected each other. They were family. They had gotten "married," and it was clear they had learned to love each other very much. I came away feeling great about church and ministry. The experience lifted my spirits and encouraged me in my work as a teacher of future ministers.

So if you have a good "marriage"—at home or at church—take care of it. Treasure it. Be thankful for it. Don't neglect it. It is a gift not to be taken for granted.

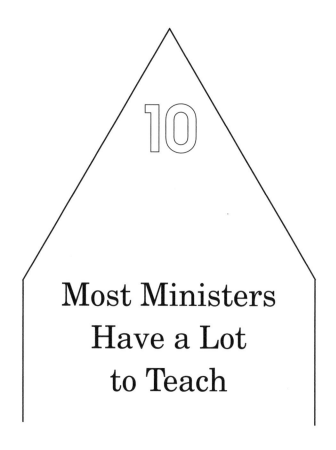

Most Ministers
Have a Lot
to Teach

A former leader of my denomination came to speak at a convocation on our campus. His topic was the renewal of the church. He said that one thing he believed was crucial for the renewal of the church was for seminary graduates to teach the Bible in their churches as if they really had been to seminary!

I thought his statement was one of those "pearls of wisdom" that said a lot in a few words. His simple challenge underscored the vital role most ministers need to have in a congregation—that of teacher. Jesus was called "rabbi," meaning teacher. I believe this is the primary role of any minister—to teach her people. Ministers are the resident theologians in their churches. They are the ones who have had the privilege of extensive and intensive study of scripture, theology, and church tradition. They are the ones equipped to lead people to the great truths of scripture that can transform people's lives. They are the ones who can help churches remain faithful covenant partners in resisting the temptations of cultural values.

There is little dispute among ministers and lay people that all of us need to know scripture better than we do. What with so many good translations of the Bible available, it is ironic that we live at a time when church members know less and less about it. This situation has to change. A church that does not know scripture—and church tradition—will lose its way. This, I fear, has already happened in the modern church. What we are talking about, then, is the recovery of our roots, to get solid ground under our feet again.

Who else can help in this task but the minister? No one has the education and training for the recovery of roots more than—or even equal to—the minister. This is the reason for theological study—to teach people the good news and responsibilities of discipleship found in scripture and informed by church tradition. Ministers are not counselors. Ministers are not administrators. Ministers are not civic leaders. Ministers are not social activists. Ministers are theologians, people who know the things of God. The ministry may involve some or all of these other things, but first and foremost ministry is teaching the things of God.

Who else can help in this task? No one! Unless the minister teaches in the church, the things of God will go untaught. Certainly lay people can assist in this ministry, but they depend upon those who have studied to guide them. I am convinced that every minister should teach a Bible class every fall and every spring at least, and more often when possible. My experience is that this is the area of ministry most neglected by ministers today. Some of them tell me that church members will not come to serious Bible study, that they want the minister to lead a "devotional" type of study without ever really engaging the biblical material.

I am sure that this is the expectation of some church members, perhaps most of them. But as a pastor I found a hunger for serious Bible study among enough members to make it worthwhile. In every church I have served I set up a series of courses that had high expectations, and offered them in cycles the way we do here at the seminary. I never had any trouble having more than enough people to fill them. We are even seeing an increase in the number of lay people who want to audit our seminary Bible courses. What is more, my colleagues say that more often than not these people are the best students they have. They come to every class session prepared to discuss the material that has been assigned. The irony is that these same people are not being offered this kind of study in their churches.

I not only believe ministers should regularly offer Bible study in their churches, I also believe that every sermon should be an exposition of scripture. Frankly, I think we have had enough of so-called topical preaching, where the minister writes out what he wants to talk about and then tries to find a scripture passage to fit it. In my opinion topical preaching has contributed no small measure to the decline of quality preaching and biblical literacy in the church. Church members need to hear the Bible preached and taught whenever there is the opportunity for it, which is usually not all that often.

I am acquainted with two churches—very different in their traditions and theological perspectives—where the ministers teach in their sermons every week. One of them even calls the preaching moments a "teaching." Both of these are alive and vibrant congregations. One of them is suburban, the other urban, which suggests that scripture can be preached regardless of the social and economic environment of the church.

I said at the beginning that most ministers have a lot to teach. Not all. Just most. Only those who spend time in study and prayer have a lot to teach. A few want to spend their time doing other things. Those other things may be important. They do not, however, provide the foundation for the church's life that is indispensable. Only prayerful meditation on the teaching of the things of God can do that. This is what most of the ministers I know want to do. This is why we entered ministry.

This is also why we spend three or more years in formal study. Being called by God for ministry is not enough to prepare one to preach and teach. Theological education is needed for ministers the same way medical education is needed for doctors. The awesome responsibility of the task before us requires the very best education we can receive. As an educator I know that seminary study has room for much improvement, but without it we would have the situation of the blind leading the blind in the church. The one who leads must first have had her eyes opened. The one who teaches must first have been taught, and then teach as if he really has been taught!

I think most ministers have a lot to teach. They may have let other things take time away from this task, but they still have a lot to teach. What is needed is the recovery of the role of teacher as a model for their ministry. There are other things to be done that have their place. None, though, can substitute for the responsibility and opportunity of teaching the things of God.

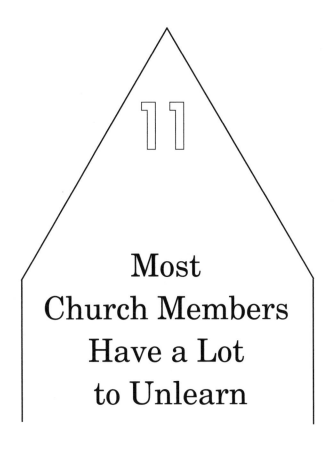

Most
Church Members
Have a Lot
to Unlearn

Socrates once said something to the effect that to know we must first unlearn what we already know. This was certainly true for me when I made the decision to enter the ministry. The first class I had in New Testament opened my mind to a world of scholarship I did not know existed. Most of what I was being taught contradicted the things I had learned growing up in the church. It made more sense to me. The Bible came alive for me. The first year of seminary was the most exciting learning experience I have ever had. It was also the most unsettling. I had to unlearn so much I had been taught about the Bible in order to experience the richness of the new world of study I was discovering.

I do not think I am an exception. For many, if not most, church members, learning the Bible—and the history of Christianity—will involve a considerable amount of unlearning. In all candor I think it is time for church leaders to admit that much of what church members have been taught for years simply is not what the Bible says. We have learned a few broad themes, such as God is love or we should love our neighbors as we love ourselves, but the particularities are woefully lacking. At the same time, much of the theology that exists among the laity is, to be candid, simply awful! Without knowing it, it is often a distortion of the Bible, if not a downright contradiction of it. What makes matters worse is that church members are found to speak these mistaken notions of what scripture says with confidence and authority. A common example is how they understand the relationship between the Old and New Testaments. I hear them say that the Old Testament is about the wrath of God, while the New Testament is about God's love.

No responsible teacher of scripture believes that. It is just not true. There is much about God's love in the Old Testament. Psalm 145, where the writer's experience of God is one of love and grace, immediately comes to mind:

> The LORD is gracious and
>   merciful,
>   Slow to anger and
>   abounding in steadfast love.
>   Psalm 145:8

This is a far cry from a God of wrath and vengeance. True, some of that is in the Old Testament, but it is also found in the New. I think of Jesus' words to unrepentant cities found in the Gospel of Matthew:

> Woe to you, Chorazin! Woe to you, Bethsaida! For if the deeds of power done in you had been done in Tyre and Sidon, they would have repented long ago in sackcloth and ashes. But I tell you, on the

day of judgment it will be more tolerable for Tyre
and Sidon than for you.

Matthew 11:21–22

In this same passage Jesus also blasts Capernaum.
Yet this is not the way Jesus always talks in the Gospels.
Indeed, the most dominant picture he paints of God is
one of a father welcoming home a lost son without ever
knowing if the son has come home to stay (Luke 15:11–
32).

The point is that most church members have a lot to
learn about the Bible that will contradict the things they
already think it says. They have tried to understand the
teachings of Jesus without any knowledge of the Judaism
that he practiced. This has served to narrow, and even
corrupt, people's understanding of Judaism and Christianity. And when it comes to church history, the vast
majority of Christians look at the history of Christianity
through rose-colored glasses. They do not know that
church history is replete with examples of Christian atroci-
ties done to "Jews and infidels," a favorite phrase used by
Christian writers, all in the name of Jesus Christ. The
Crusades of the Middle Ages were only a drop in the
bucket when it came to Christian persecution of non-
Christians.

The average church member knows little, if anything
at all, about biblical scholarship of the last two hundred
years, or of church history over the last two thousand.
Instead, church members know bits and pieces of things
they have heard in sermons or were taught in Sunday
school that have prejudiced them against the genuine
truth of God in scripture and history. When I hear all the
"stuff" people say in church, supposedly based upon the
Bible, I tend to become discouraged about the challenge
before us. I remember hearing as a child in my native
South church folk saying blacks (and they didn't use that
word) were cursed by God through the curse of Cain.
Apparently they had never read the story of Cain and
Abel for themselves. Otherwise they would have known

that the mark God put on Cain was not a curse but a blessing. It was intended to protect him, "lest any one who came upon him should kill him" (Genesis 4:15).

This may be an extreme case, but it points to the problem. Church members have much to unlearn before they can ever learn what scripture and church tradition teach. I learned early in seminary that I had to let go of much that I believed about the Bible in order to learn for the first time what the Bible really had to say. What I thought I knew was a barrier to learning. At first I rebelled. I thought the warning of some of the members of my home church not to let "those teachers" destroy my faith was coming true. It was only as this "new" way of studying scripture strengthened and deepened my faith that I knew my home church members were speaking out of "knowledge" that *they* had to unlearn.

The truth is, there is a lot of bad theology in the church today that needs to be jettisoned if the church is ever to hear the gospel of Jesus Christ in its fullest and richest measure. This is not to suggest that what people believe makes them a good or bad Christian. We know, of course, it is what they do that ultimately matters. On this score many church members come out ahead. But often what we do is determined by what we believe. What we believe will not save us. Only the grace of God can do that. It can, on the other hand, keep us from repeating a lot of mistakes Christians have made in the past. What we believe, therefore, does matter. Knowledge matters. And the quality of the knowledge we are gaining makes a difference in how well we live.

What we face in the church today is the task of having to unlearn much of what we think we know in order to be open to the truth of God that can set us free from the mistakes and barriers that have undercut the church's witness in the world. This is a "hard" word to most church members. It is also one that is unavoidable for Jesus' sake.

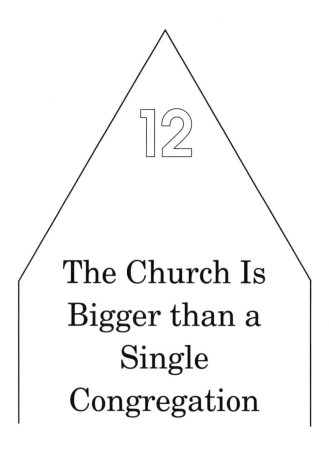

The Church Is Bigger than a Single Congregation

In my denomination we often remind ourselves of a basic conviction of our tradition, which is, "We are Christians only, but not the only Christians." We do not always act as if we believe these words. Yet they have been formative in our history. They affirm our conviction that we belong to Jesus Christ, while also acknowledging that he does not belong to us. As a people who have been and continue to be committed to the ecumenical vision of church, holding in tension being Christians only, but not being the only Christians is central to our identity and mission.

It took us a long time to confess that we had evolved over the years into another North American denomination. It was not what our founders had in mind in the

early 1800s. They believed they could transcend denominationalism by focusing on the New Testament system of
faith and design for the church and unite all Christians
into one church. They called denominationalism the "scan-
dal of Christianity." That is why we functioned like a
denomination for many years before we admitted to ourselves in 1968 that we had joined the rest of mainline
Protestantism in becoming one. Before that we called
ourselves "the brotherhood." At least candor about what
we had become moved us away from using an identity
label that left out over half the members of our church—
namely women. But the confession was a painful re-
minder that we were far from realizing the dream with
which we had begun as a people—to be a spark that
united all Christians into one body.

Yet the vision has not been lost. The work for Christian unity has not been abandoned, and is now shared by
every major Protestant body. But the quest for Christian
unity has required adaptation to changing conditions.
Churches working together in an ecumenical spirit is one
such adaptation. While the road to the church of Christ
on earth healing its divisions to the point of visible union
remains a long and difficult one, church members have
realized that all churches and all denominations can at
least be ecumenical, can at least confess together that we
are Christians only, but not the only Christians. The
alternative to being an ecumenical Christian and an ecumenical church is sectarianism, which is to believe that
we are the only Christians, and anyone who wants to be a
Christian has to be like us.

I know a few church members who believe this way—
but only a few. Most church members across denominational lines are quick to reject this kind of narrow-
mindedness. The fact that people move with ease from
one denomination to another suggests that sectarianism
does not dominate mainline church life today. At the
same time, though, I do not know many church members
who believe the ecumenical witness of the church is worth
much of their time and financial support. They act as if
the word *ecumenical* is Greek to them. If there is any-

thing to which we seem to give lip service, it is the ecumenical vision of church. I would be the first to admit that I am as guilty of doing this as anyone. I have always believed in the ecumenical movement. I just never have devoted much attention to it. It was something I let others work at, while I "prayed" for them (but not really).

This is ironic, because every time I hear someone speak who has an ecumenical vision my understanding of the church is deepened and broadened. A neighboring seminary recently invited Emilio Castro, former general secretary of the World Council of Churches, to speak. As I listened to him talk about his experiences in the world-wide church, I knew he was speaking about the ministry of Christ in the world on a scale that no single denomination could possibly sustain on its own. Only as churches of many different traditions cooperate on a global basis can the church witness the way it does. Moreover, I have no doubt that this kind of ecumenical vision is consistent with, if not a prerequisite of, the church becoming one as Christ prayed for us to be (John 17). Indeed, being ecumenical goes beyond cooperating with other Christians. It is a way of being Christian, as individuals and congregations.

We are fortunate at our seminary to have two members of our faculty who are leaders in the ecumenical work of the whole church. The problem, though, is that the ecumenical vision of the church does not seem to make much difference to local church members. The ones I know do not get very excited about it. They are not against ecumenical concerns. Many of them attend seasonal community ecumenical worship services, and support joint missions such as food banks and soup kitchens. Beyond these activities most church members seem quite content with denominationalism.

I believe ecumenical leaders have contributed to this situation by working primarily on denominational levels of the church, far removed from local congregations. But there are new efforts to change this situation. One of my colleagues is leading a program of asking local congregation to become "faith partners" in ecumenical ministry with the World Council of Churches, naming and identifying many things local congregations already affirm. This program has several dimensions, but the underlying conviction is that the ecumenical vision of church life can contribute to the health and well-being of local congregations. Through tangible partnership the ecumenical movement can make a contribution to the renewal of the church. My other colleague believes the ecumenical movement holds great potential for strengthening local congregations, if it can be understood as historically being a renewal movement itself.

In those moments when I experience a renewal of my own spirit, when I "catch" a little bit of the ecumenical vision, I understand what he means. It seems only reasonable to believe that the personal renewal I experience can happen in a local congregation. In a time when mainline churches are searching for paths to renewal, it may be that the ecumenical vision of the church is in a *kairos* time in potential for renewing modern church life. Limiting our vision of the church to the local congregation of which we are a part certainly diminishes our appreciation of what God is doing in the world.

Just as the world is so much bigger than the local community where we live, so is the church. It seems to me that it will take a global church to confront the needs and issues that go with living in a global community. It is tempting to try to withdraw from the larger world community into the security of our little world. But I think most church members know that is not a realistic way to live anymore. I think ecumenical leaders today are telling us that we can be engaged in the global church as we work in our local congregations, if we remember that we are not only members of a local church. It is true that we can only work where we are. At the same time, we can know that we are being represented by Christians working in other places, even as we represent them in our work. This kind of thinking helps them to be a part of us and us to be a part of them. I believe this kind of attitude can contribute in a real way to new life in mainline churches. May it be so.

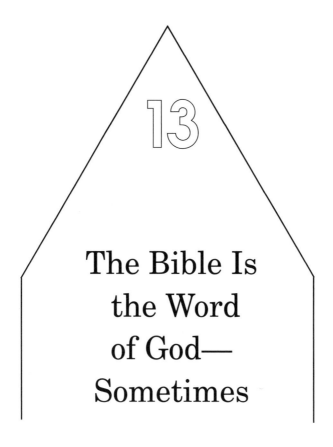

The Bible Is
the Word
of God—
Sometimes

At the end of the reading of scripture in the worship of some churches, the reader will say, "The word of the Lord," to which the people respond, "Thanks be to God." Even though I do not come from this type of liturgical tradition, I like it. It is a significant moment in a congregation's life to declare to themselves that the scripture they have just heard is the word of the Lord for their lives.

But what does it really mean to say that the Bible is the word of God? Some church members want to make it a legalistic confession, sort of a "sign on the dotted line" statement that makes one's faith legitimate. There are even some seminaries nowadays that are requiring faculty members to sign a statement that declares they believe the Bible is the inspired word of God. Frankly, though, I think this misses the point. Worse than that, it comes close to trivializing scripture by turning its statements of faith into doctrines to determine orthodoxy. It is not a new thing for the church, but every time it occurs more damage than good is done.

The reason I say this is quite simple. The Bible cannot be the word of God for or to anyone who will not listen to it. Say whatever we want to, threaten people with the fires of hell, rant and rave, but none of it will make one whit of difference to the indifferent. Moreover, I do not think one has to be outside the church for this to be the case. There are more than a few church members who do not listen to scripture any more than nonchurch members. Their lives are closed to the transforming truth of the Bible, as if they have never read or heard a passage of scripture. And if we take sin seriously, then the only honest confession any of us can make is that all of us are in the same boat. Not one of us listens to scripture without selective hearing.

It seems to me the truth of the Bible is something that does not need the church's defense. The church existed and flourished for centuries before it ever had what we today consider the canon of scripture. Not that we do not need to have the Bible. We do! Of course we do. It is, as I have already said, the foundation and guide for the church's life. But it is that foundation and guide, it seems to me, when and only when church members choose to make it the word of the Lord for and in their lives. No one can force the truth of scripture on another. The church has already tried that and failed. The truth of scripture does its own convincing. That is an experience nothing can make happen, and nothing can change when it does.

Personally I believe scripture is too inspired and too sacred to be bogged down in church fights over who "really" believes in the Bible and who doesn't. The power of the Word is of God, not the church, and not what the church says about the Word. I will confess that there are times when I read scripture—and hear it read—and it does little for me. There are other times, though, when it becomes a transforming message from the Lord for my life, and I am not the same because of it.

I believe the folks who want to declare that the Bible is the inspired word of God, and have everyone else agree with them, mean well. But I still think they are missing the point. What matters is what happens in my life and yours when we do hear the Bible as the word of the Lord. Even if scripture is the word of the Lord only sometimes, when it is it can make all the difference in the world.

As a pastor I cared little about having a church full of people who would stand firm in their conviction that the Bible was the inspired word of God. What I really wanted was a church full of people who, when the morning lessons were read on Sunday, and the reader would end by saying, "The word of the Lord," they could respond in sincerity and trust by saying, "Thanks be to God." Such a church is one whose members know the Bible as the word of the Lord for their lives. In that way it has become inspired and holy.

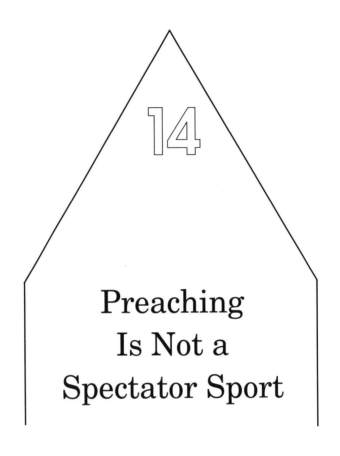

Preaching
Is Not a
Spectator Sport

I do not know a church anywhere that does not want a good preacher. Many churches have ministers whose strength does not lie in the pulpit, but all churches appreciate good preaching and hope with each change in ministerial leadership to get someone who can do it. The president of our seminary has been traveling extensively in recent months among churches and individuals on behalf of the seminary's capital campaign. He said the first thing people invariably say to him is, "Graduate some good preachers."

Ministers also appreciate good preaching. I have never met a minister who did not want to be a good preacher. I know some who are candid enough to admit that they aren't, but they would like to be, and they enjoy hearing a good sermon. I have also known a few who thought they were, but nobody else thought so. The chair of a search committee told me not long ago that they requested a taped sermon from a prospective minister who listed preaching as one of his strengths. The committee unanimously agreed after listening to the tape that the minister either had an inflated notion of the quality of his preaching or poor judgment regarding which taped sermon to send them.

I hope we have gotten beyond all the talk about preaching being dead. There certainly has been a lot of dead preaching in the church, but good preaching is alive and well. It would be hard to overstate the importance of good preaching in the life of a congregation. Having said that, though, it seems to me that many church members do not understand what makes for good preaching Sunday after Sunday. Preparation and study on the part of the minister are indispensable, to be sure. A good sermon does not write itself. The idea that all a preacher has to do is open the Bible and start preaching and the Spirit will give her the words to say is foolishness. I don't believe for a minute that God will rescue me—or anyone else—from the irresponsibility of no preparation. One might hope that the Spirit would be at work doing damage control. That is the most one could hope for.

The preparation done by the minister, however, is not the sole factor in good preaching. Nor is it his skill in oral communication. Quality of delivery helps, is even indispensable. But something else is involved in good preaching. It is the participation of the congregation in the preaching moment. Nothing substitutes for a congregation of people who have anticipated the sermon as a moment when the word of the Lord will be proclaimed, and they are anxious to hear it. Nothing substitutes for a congregation of people who show in their faces and in their responses that they are listening intently to what is being said. Nothing substitutes for a congregation of people who sit on the edge of their seats, waiting for the next word from the preacher that just might change their lives.

Am I making too much over the preaching moment? I do not think so. Can ministers live up to this kind of active participation in preaching? Frankly, I do not think a congregation will ever know until they try it. I am sorry to say that my experience tells me that most have not. More accurate is the picture of church members who approach the time for the sermon with polite attentiveness at best, and utter boredom at worst. This may be because of bitter experience. I think a more likely cause for this attitude toward the preaching moment on Sunday is the fact that church members think of themselves as spectators of the sermon. They are there to listen, which they interpret to mean being passive.

Listening does not have to be passive. Listening does not mean being a spectator to what is going on. Everyone knows the difference in the feeling we have when we are talking to someone who makes it clear they are listening, and the feeling we have when it is clear the person is not listening to anything we are saying. Their response, their participation, will energize and encourage us to say what we really want to say, or it will discourage and frustrate us to the point where we do not want to say anything.

I may not be the best preacher around, but I work long and hard at it. Hardly a Sunday passes that I am not preaching somewhere. For years I did it every Sunday as a local church pastor. No one will ever convince me that the way church members listen does not help or hinder good preaching. Black preachers know this very well. Their church members speak right back to them. It makes a difference.

Years ago I was preaching a revival in a church in my hometown. My cousin and her husband attended one of the services. He was a Pentecostal minister. As I preached, he began to respond with "Amen." I knew my cousin was a bit uneasy about it, since it was not the tradition of my denomination to do this. But I loved it! I felt empowered and encouraged as he responded. I knew at least one person was listening, and that made me want to give the best that was in me in that sermon.

Speaking back to the preacher is not the only way church members can participate in the preaching moment. Nonverbal communication speaks as loud as words. I can tell when a person is listening to me while I am preaching, without them having to say a word. When I was a pastor I would sometimes tell my people that I wished they could stand where I was standing and see the looks on their faces. It was enough to discourage the best of preachers!

Everybody wants good preaching. What many church members do not know is that good preaching needs everybody's participation. When I first graduated from seminary, my regional minister—someone in my denomination who functions somewhat like a bishop—told me that he wanted me to go to a particular church because they would make a good preacher out of me. What he meant was that they expected good preaching, and helped the minister make it happen. Church members can do that more than they believe. Many things go into good preaching, some of them intangible and immeasurable. The anticipation and participation of the congregation is one of them. Whatever else preaching is, it is not a spectator sport.

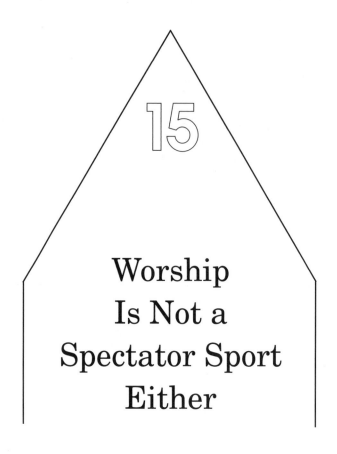

Worship
Is Not a
Spectator Sport
Either

Being spectators at a sermon is symptomatic of the way many church members think about worship as a whole. It is a time to be passive, to be "done to," so to speak. A spectator understanding of worship nurtures, or at best gives permission to, church members seeing their role in the worship life of a church as the "critic." The quality and place of everything in a worship service has to pass only one test—"Do I like it?" Often they waste no time telling others when they don't. Unfortunately, they seldom say anything when they do.

I confess to a bit of bashing here, but anyone who has participated in the planning and leading of worship knows what I am talking about. Somewhere along the way church members have gotten the impression that worship is for us. Wrong! Worship is not for us. It is for God. The one who needs to be "pleased" with our worship is God, not us. Someone—I think it was Danish theologian Søren Kierkegaard—once described worship as a great drama in which church members are on stage and God is the audience. His point was that worship is our offering to God, not the minister's offering to the members.

In the book *Pastoral Theology*, which we require all first-year students to read, Thomas Oden writes about worship this way:

> It is God whom we worship. We gather not to worship ourselves, our desperate struggles for God, our hunger for God, or our immediate feelings for God, but nothing less than God alone, who awakens our thirst for [God's] presence and who stands at the beginning and end of our struggles, hungers and feelings. We worship not a political ideal, not a local community, not a family, not an economic system, but God the giver of all of these possibilities. Worship that does not address God, listen to God, speak to God, is not Christian worship.[1]

I believe church members who understand worship in this way will come to church not as spectators, but ready and anxious to participate in worship. The hymns and songs will be viewed as opportunities for praise. Prayers will be moments of intimate communion with God. The sermon will be heard with hearts full of anticipation that a word from the Lord will be spoken. The offering will be a chance to put our money where we say our heart is. The communion will be a sacred moment when we relive, in the act of remembering, the grace of God revealed in the death and resurrection of Jesus Christ.

What an exciting time worship in the church would be if members did not "spectate" and instead focused on ways to express gratitude to and love for God. How different the atmosphere in worship would be if church members had the attitude that they were not present to be pleased, but to please the only one who needs pleasing.

The renewal of the church is a topic under much discussion in our seminary. One conviction upon which we have been able to agree is that renewal will always include a renewal of the worship life of the church. A church whose worship is boring and dead is a boring and dead church. The seeds of boring and dead worship grow up in the soil of attitudes among church members that they are spectators on Sunday morning much the way they are on Sunday afternoon watching football. Experience has convinced me that when church members focus on pleasing God, their worship life dramatically increases in quality and inspiration. New ideas about worship are welcomed with the hope of holding a new expression of thankful praise in God.

We learned this in my last congregation from a Southern Baptist church that understood the purpose and meaning of genuine Christian worship. My first experience in worship with this congregation challenged my long-held beliefs about worship. After more visits I realized I thought about worship in self-centered terms, what I liked and did not like, a problem I believe most ministers have. We think the worship service is "ours." I learned from this Baptist church how wrong and harmful that is. Some months later several other members from our church attended services at the Baptist church, and then attended a weekend workshop. It permanently changed the way we thought about worship, eventually giving direction to the planning and quality of the worship life at our own church.

One of the things we discovered is that when we stopped focusing on what we wanted and started focusing on ways to praise God, our own needs in worship began being met. Services became exciting and inspiring. Our spirits were lifted, our minds challenged, and our sense of oneness as a people deepened. For the first time we started thinking about why we did what we did. In the midst of weekly changes, worship began to have a discernible flow and direction that held it together. It was both ordered and flexible. There was formality in an atmosphere of freedom and spontaneity. Focusing on God was the way worship took on meaning for us.

It is such a simple thing to focus on God and not on ourselves in worship. It may not be easy to determine what is pleasing to God and what is not. But that is not the problem with worship in most churches. The problem is that we think worship is for us. And we want what we want. We may have some theological justification for what we want, but it is still what we want. We are there to be pleased, and even to be entertained. Most of all we are there to watch, to judge, to critique, to spectate. If, on the other hand, we think of worship as our offering to God, then watching and judging and spectating are not possible. For to try to please God requires all our energies as we seek to serve rather than to be served. Churches that have members who understand who worship is for, who is to be pleased, and who is to do the pleasing are churches whose worship hour redeems and renews those who make their offerings to God.

[1]Thomas Oden, *Pastoral Theology* (Harper & Row, 1983), p. 94.

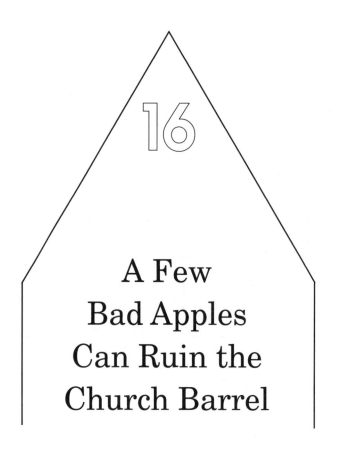

A Few Bad Apples Can Ruin the Church Barrel

How many church members does it take to make a ministry work? All of them! How many does it take to tear one down? Sometimes only one. It takes the best efforts of all church members to build a strong ministry. It only takes a few to tear it down. A few church members can fuss and gripe and pick and complain until the spirit has been drained from everyone else. At that point ministry becomes impossible.

It is true that no one can please everyone. It is also true that the complaints of church members are sometimes justified. What I'm talking about are the few individuals in churches who seem to take it upon themselves to pick at everyone and everything that goes on. These people are unhappy, and they seem determined to try to make everyone else unhappy. Nothing pleases them. Sometimes they will become upset over something that is said or done, and they just can't wait to let everyone know about it.

More than once I have seen such people try to gather support around their point of view, which usually means creating dissatisfaction with the current ministerial leadership of the church. Unless the lay leadership takes a strong stand in support of the minister(s), a few people can bring a good ministry to a premature end. Before that happens, though, they can take all the joy out of church life. The spirit of those in leadership dims gradually, and finally dries up.

I had the experience in my last pastorate of a few people acting like this who were not even members of the church. They had been members of one of the Sunday school classes for many years, but had never joined the church. Seldom, if ever, did they attend worship. Yet that did not stop them from resisting changes we were making in the church's life and ministry, especially in the worship service. Moreover, they had no hesitation in letting everybody in their class know how they felt. They were not successful in garnering the support they wanted for their views, but they did manage to make life miserable for our entire church staff. Every week we found ourselves on the phone or in a meeting trying to answer the complaints these people were making about what we were trying to do.

It is easy enough for those who support a ministry to tell their minister(s), "Don't let them get to you." It's just not that easy to do. Nobody wants to do ministry where they constantly have to deal with an undercurrent of dissatisfaction and tension. Ministers worth their salt will eventually decide that life is too short for that. In the end a few people will have ruined a ministry that was good for most of the other members.

I am not advocating that people like this be thrown out of the church. At the same time, church members who care about the church have to face the hard truth that these people do serious harm to a church's life and ministry. No church can be all things to all people. At some point a person has to decide whether or not they want to share life with a particular congregation. If they won't make that decision, then the church has to force the issue. It is not "un-Christian" to tell someone that if they cannot work with the rest of the people for the common welfare of the church, then they should seek to find a place where they can.

The elders in my last pastorate did that on two occasions. They were very pastoral in their approach, but they stood firm in their support for the direction the ministry was going. They knew most of the people were excited about the new life the church was experiencing. These two people in particular were trying to undercut it. Finally, after many months of discussion, the elders decided that they should make it clear to these people that they were welcomed to stay, if they would stop their destructive ways. Otherwise, they needed to find a new church home.

I shared this experience in one of my classes. One student was shocked at what we did. She thought we had no right to say anything to these people. After all, we were supposed to love everyone in the church. Her heart was in the right place, but she was incredibly naive about the toughness of ministry. The reality is that it does take everyone to make a ministry strong and only a few to tear one down. There is such a thing as "tough love" in the church. Loving others does not require us to sacrifice the common good for the sake of a few people. The whole barrel has a right to protect itself against the damage a few bad apples can do. That is reality. I also happen to believe it is responsible stewardship of church life.

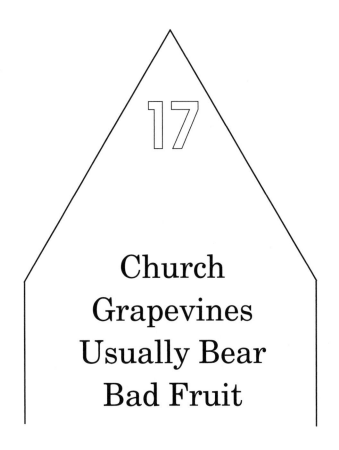

Church Grapevines Usually Bear Bad Fruit

A church grapevine, to put it bluntly, is the network of gossip that seems to exist in every church. In all my years of ministry I have never seen anything good come from a church grapevine. On the contrary, it has always been a destructive and sinful force in the life of a church.

I believe there is no worse sin than gossip. Its effect is always—without exception—negative and disruptive to individuals and the congregation as a whole. It expresses the worst of us as human beings—our insensitivity to others, our tendency to prejudge situations and people or to judge without cause, the arrogance of seeing the speck in another's eye without seeing the planks in our own, and the inability to control our tongues, all the while pretending ignorance of its damage. Nothing is worse that the sin of gossip, especially in the church where people are called to share life in Christ.

Church grapevines almost always thrive on gossip. People love to talk, and many church members do so without concerning themselves with the accuracy, or even the truthfulness, of their information. Moreover, the embellishing of stories that contain a kernel of truth is appalling. Even spreading stories that are true can be destructive. The telling lacks compassion and concern because the telling is the focus of the teller's attention. Whenever the person(s) who is (are) the subject of the story is (are) not the primary focus of concern, what is being told—true or false—is gossip.

The Letter of James talks about the evil and damage of the church grapevine this way:

> The tongue is a fire. The tongue is placed among our members as a world of iniquity, strains the whole body, sets on fire the cycle of nature, and is itself set on fire by hell....With it we bless the Lord and Father, and with it we curse those who are made in the likeness of God. From the same mouth come blessing and cursing....This ought not to be so.
>
> James 3:6–10

Most church members will readily agree that gossip is a terrible thing, while at the same time engaging in it or at least tolerating it in the life of their church. It is as if they do not believe it actually destroys the way it does. Perhaps the reason church grapevines are tolerated is because the messages they carry are not recognized as gossip. After all, the talk is not usually about some moral indiscretion of another church member, although whenever such indiscretions do occur they certainly make the circuit. Most often, though, the grapevine in the church carries inaccurate and distorted information about what happened in the board meeting or some committee of the church. It is quite common for it to be a carrier for the opinions of a disgruntled church member who wants everyone to know her dissatisfaction with the minister.

In one church I served there was one particular Sunday school class that made sure the church grapevine was kept busy. The members were an aging group who truly loved the church, but their understanding of church life was skewed in significant ways. There was very little we did in ministry that they supported. Every week the church staff could count on someone in the class passing along information about something we had said or done that was inaccurate or completely untrue. Yet not once did any of them ever come to us and ask whether or not what they had heard was true. It was as if the talking itself were more important than truth.

It may be obvious by now that I have no patience with church grapevines, nor any respect for them. They hurt people and they damage churches. What is worse, there is simply too much tolerance for them. In the name of not wanting to hurt anyone's feelings, churches will let people gossip without challenging the act itself. Members may take issue with a statement that has been made, but they seldom ask the person talking why they are gossiping. This is what needs to be done. There is no place in the church for loose tongues. I think James puts the matter of a loose tongue in the church rather bluntly: "This ought not to be so."

It really is not all that difficult to stop a church grapevine. All we need to do when confronted with gossip is to make it perfectly clear that we don't want to hear it—period! This needs to be our response especially when there is trouble in a church. That is when the grapevine is most alive, and most inaccurate. At such times even the smallest problems grow into big ones, adding to the tension that already exists.

Nothing good ever comes from a church grapevine, which is why church members concerned about the health and well-being of their church should never let it go unchallenged. No one can stop people from gossiping. We

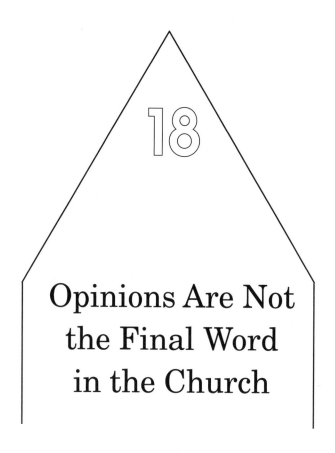

Opinions Are Not the Final Word in the Church

There is a general attitude in the church that everyone is entitled to his opinion, no matter how outrageous it may be. We view this freedom as basic to being Americans. Freedom to one's opinion is basic to our way of life. It is called freedom of speech, the First Amendment of the U.S. Constitution.

What may come as a shock to a lot of church members is that in a real sense freedom of speech, being entitled to one's opinion, does not exist in the church. All church members can, of course, hold any opinion they want to. No member should try to limit another from speaking her convictions. I am not suggesting that there should be a single theological point of view that would be binding on everyone. Indeed, my own denominational polity is congregational autonomy, which over the years has come to mean that no one tells anyone what to think or do or believe or how to act. I like the freedom my tradition values and protects. But it is not the last word in the church.

The last word in the church is not personal opinion. Church members have a more demanding obligation than personal opinions by the very nature of their membership in the church. Personal opinion is not the highest, nor even the noblest, value in the church. What matters most—in fact, the only thing that really does matter in the church—is the will of God. Any opinion we have as church members pales in comparison to knowing and doing the will of God.

Somewhere along the line we got it in our heads that the church is a democracy. Well, it isn't. The church is a theocracy. Human opinion and will are subservient to divine will. What we think matters only as we try to understand what God thinks. Granted, that is no easy task, and consensus about God's will is hardly something easy to achieve. That there are differences among church members over what the will of God is in specific situations is normal and healthy to the life of the church. The problem is when the attempt to discern the divine will is ignored or neglected. It often is. There have been precious few church board meetings I have attended during my ministry where seeking to know the will of God regarding an important decision has even been mentioned. People usually state their opinions, a vote is taken, the "ayes" have it, and we move on to the next item. God's will is the majority opinion of those present and voting!

We talk a lot about doing God's will, but unless we take the time to know it—within the obvious limitations of human discernment—doing God's will becomes little more than doing what we want to do in the name of God's will. At its worst that borders on taking God's name in vain. At its best it is human wisdom at work. In both cases the honest seeking after God's will is secondary to our wants and desires.

As difficult as knowing God's will is, it is not as if we are completely adrift in its pursuit. At our disposal are rich resources of discernment. The most obvious one is scripture. I suspect the quality of church life would rise significantly and the extent of Christian mission would increase dramatically, if members studied scripture in the context of making decisions about their church's life and mission.

Consider, for example, the tragedy of homelessness. There can be no debate what the teaching of scripture says about our response to the homeless. They are the widows and orphans of the Torah story and the stranger in the ditch on the road to Jericho in the parables of Jesus. They are our neighbors. In light of scripture, there is only one question church members need to ask—"How do we help them?" In many churches, though, when the problem is discussed the question focuses on *if* church members will do anything. Comments such as, "Many of these people want to be on the street," or, "A lot of them are alcoholics," are common. These are opinions of church members. They think they have a right to them. I want to suggest that they have a higher obligation, which is to weigh what they think against what they honestly believe scripture has to say.

Church tradition also has much to say in helping us discern the will of God. The church was not born yesterday. The history of the people of God reaches back hundreds of years. Those who went before us faced many of the dilemmas we face. Their wisdom and experience can give guidance to our thinking and acting If nothing else, we can learn from their mistakes. Who was it who said that those who do not learn from the mistakes of the past are destined to repeat them?

This is not to say that circumstances today are no different from days passed. They are, to be sure. But we have a history as the people of God. We have scripture and church tradition that offer us wisdom and guidance.

We also have the wisdom of contemporary thinkers schooled in the advances of modern knowledge that builds upon the wisdom of the past. It is not enough to have an opinion. I tell my students that everyone is entitled to an opinion, but there are a lot of stupid opinions around! All opinions do not carry the same weight. Some are informed and some are not. I think the only opinions that ought to matter in the church are those that are rooted in a person's honest effort to know the will of God. There will be differences of opinion on what the will of God is. That we should be seeking the divine will, however, is not in dispute. Doing God's will and not our own is what being church members is all about. This is why human opinions alone are not the final word in the church.

19

You Can't Take out of a Person's Mind with Reason What Reason Did Not Put into It in the First Place

I heard the late Methodist bishop, Gerald Kennedy, say this many years ago. I have never forgotten it. It is practical advice at its best. I think of how much better off all of us in the church would be if we remembered what he said. In the previous chapter I talked about opinions not being the final word in the church. In urging church members to subject their personal opinions to what they understand the will of God to be, I recognize my challenge flies in the face of the late bishop's wisdom. That people do not give up their opinions quickly is directly related to the fact that many times reason is not why they hold them in the first place.

As a native southerner I saw first hand the ugliness of racism. I am convinced that racism is never a reasoned response to racial differences. More than anything else it is rooted in cultural conditioning that has exploited fear and ignorance. I do not remember any overt expressions of racism in my home as a youth. What I do remember is that we called one of my playmates who was black "Sonny Boy." I also remember that he could never come inside our house when all the rest of us went in to eat lunch. He would have to eat on the back porch. Years later I met "Sonny Boy" when he and I were grown men. For the first time in my life I found out his real name was Walter Fore.

I can hardly believe we called Walter "Sonny Boy." I am ashamed. Yet there are people I grew up with who to this day reject any suggestion that calling Walter Fore "Sonny Boy" was—or is—an expression of racism. Walter told me that a very prominent minister we grew up with persists in calling him "Sonny Boy." Walter has expressed his displeasure about the name, but this old childhood friend thinks Walter is being too sensitive, that it's just "foolin' around."

Apparently this man never thinks about at whose expense he is "foolin' around." I suspect the reason is precisely what Bishop Kennedy was talking about. Reason did not put the racist name into the minister's mind, and reason cannot take it out. It could, of course, if the minister really would take the time to "think" about what he was saying. But, then, that would require a degree of reason that was not present in the first place.

One reason I think Bishop Kennedy's words are so important is because the church is the one place where one would hope reason would guide people's words and behavior. We have voluntarily accepted a higher claim on our lives than cultural conditioning. We claim the name of Jesus Christ. The integrity of that claim rests on our will to allow the power of Christ's presence to shape and influence what we think and do. Such shaping and influencing goes beyond reason, but certainly includes it. The key is having the will to use our minds in service to God. Church members who are serious about their Christian commitment do not cling to unreasoned views. Instead they recognize them for what they really are—unreasoned. We are living at a time when a reasoned faith is a pressing need. Issues such as AIDS, racism, sexual lifestyles and practices, hunger and starvation, the distribution of wealth, and environmental protection cannot be ignored by our society. I happen to believe the church's voice should be heard in the discussions on these concerns. But it will be ignored if church members demonstrate that they cannot discuss these issues among themselves in a reasonable way. In all candor, I am not sure that we can.

My denomination, to cite one example of why I am skeptical, is presently embroiled in controversy over the ordination of homosexuals, as are most denominations. Two years ago this controversy became focused on a colleague of mine who was the nominee for our denomination's top elected post. He is a man of integrity and commitment. His views of the church are both scriptural and visionary. He was offering our church exciting leadership potential. Yet his nomination was defeated because he believes sexual preference should not be the sole criterion for judging a person worthy or unworthy for ordination. In retrospect it is clear that no amount of reasoning—of which there was considerable effort—had much impact on the response of those who opposed him. The fact that our particular polity leaves the decision for ordination in hands outside the authority of the office for which he was nominated, essentially leaving him without authority on the issue, made no difference to them. Neither did his acknowledgment that he knew his views probably did not represent the majority of our church membership, and that, if elected, he would respect that fact.

Never has the wisdom of Bishop Kennedy's observation been so apparent to me than now. Reason certainly has its limitations. My own mother is a case in point. The newspaper in my hometown in Virginia ran a headline about my friend's nomination that said, "Pro Gay Minister Nominated for Church Post." A few days later I received a long letter from Mother in which she lamented the state of our church, which was ready to elect such a person to its top leadership position. I called her to talk about the situation. It was clear that reason was not getting me anywhere. Finally I decided to appeal to her emotions. I said to her: "Mother, if you read an article in the paper about me that had statements in it you knew were inaccurate or untrue, and if people who had never met me or heard me speak and had only read things I was supposed to have said, called me names and questioned my Christian commitment, how would that make you feel?" It was only then that she began to listen to anything I had to say about my friend.

The reason reasoning alone is often ineffective in helping people to think through what they already believe is because what is making them believe some of the things they believe is fear. They are afraid to give in to reason for fear that they will have nowhere to stand if they give up what they already believe, no matter how unreasonable what they believe may be.

Anyone who is a leader in the church needs to be realistic about what makes people think, believe and act the way they do. I once thought I could change people's minds about things in the church if they would give me a chance to reason with them. Sometimes that has, in fact, made a difference. More often than not, though, it hasn't. Reason may help, but reason alone will not change people's minds. I do not know why it took me so long to realize this. I should know it from the way I act. I am no different from anyone else. This is why developing a pastoral relationship with people is essential for any minister who wants to challenge the status quo of the church. It offers one practical way to break through the "unreasoned" beliefs some church members cling to that hurt the church's life and ministry. When people feel like you care about them, they will sometimes listen when they otherwise would not.

This is one of the first things we try to teach seminary students about ministry. Surveys have confirmed what common sense told wise ministers a long time ago. Knowing their pastor cares about them is a high priority among church members. That is the basis for building the trust between church members and ministers that is so important in the church. It would be nice if people would think and act because they have reasoned through issues. That is the case in many instances. It is why we have made progress on important issues through the ages. But it is not always the way people think and act, and it is not the way any of us think and act all the time. All of us think and act in unreasonable ways some of the time. We all have our blind spots.

Knowing that we cannot take out of a person's mind with reason what reason did not put into it in the first place is not a cause for dismay. It is simply a way to understand why they—and we—think and act at certain times about certain things.

The Common Good
Is What
Really Counts

There is a verse of scripture every church member should memorize. It is 1 Corinthians 12:7: "To each is given the manifestation of the Spirit for the common good." The Christians in Corinth did not think about the common good. They were caught up in their individual worlds. What was good for the whole was less important than what was good for the individual. They had no sense of community; no sense of the oneness of the church Jesus had prayed for (John 17:22). What they ended up with was a divided church that could not witness to Jesus Christ.

The message the apostle Paul tried to get them to hear was that they needed to work together. They needed

76

to make individual concerns and desires and beliefs secondary to the well-being of the whole church. The "common good" was the theme he underscored. His counsel regarding the exercising of the gifts of the Holy Spirit grew out of this concern. Whatever gift one might exercise, for Paul the primary concern was that it benefit more than the individual. Even the famous love chapter (1 Corinthians 13) was a challenge to get them to put the common good first. In it Paul makes his conviction clear that unconditional love could be the foundation for putting the common good first. It was a tangible way to show love for one another.

Concern for the common good is a pressing need in the modern church. It plays no small part in a church member's attitude about change. But concern for the common good is not a natural impulse for church members. We live at a time when excessive individualism dominates our culture, as Robert Bellah and his associates argue so persuasively in *Habits of the Heart*. Americans are willing to work together to a point. That point is when individual freedom has to be compromised. We believe individual freedom is absolute, the true mark of American democracy. The National Rifle Association has built a powerful political lobby on this kind of thinking. The problem is that when individual freedom becomes absolute, the common good often gets little more than lip service, and sometimes is undercut completely.

One of the leading laymen in my denomination is J. Irwin Miller, founder and president of Cummins Engine Company. A graduate of both Yale and Oxford Universities, Mr. Miller has combined a successful business career with committed church membership. In a college commencement address I once heard him deliver, he gave a disturbing example of the trouble people today have in being committed to the common good:

A young MBA has the strongest possible feeling as to the strategic program the corporation should adopt. He makes his pitch to management, and, after hearing him out, management rejects his program and chooses another.

Does our MBA, in commitment to his peers and the enterprise, then work with all his heart for the chosen plan to do what he can to make it a success? More often than not, our MBA feels no commitment at all. After all, it wasn't "his" plan. Let "them" make it work if they can. He disparages "their" plan to his peers, gives lukewarm or perhaps no cooperation in its implementation, and will be secretly overjoyed if it fails. He feels little commitment to anything other than himself.

It is not unusual to find the attitude of Mr. Miller's MBA in many church members today. They don't know how to lose with grace any better than the young businessman did. Let an issue come up and if they don't get their way they won't let it go. They keep beating a dead horse, even when it becomes very destructive to the whole church. Sometimes they will threaten to withhold financial support or withdraw from the church altogether, putting themselves ahead of what is good for all concerned.

I sometimes run into this attitude in churches in regard to women in ministry. About 40 percent of our student body are women. Most of our student churches do not want a woman for a pastor, even though our denomination has been ordaining women since its beginning. There are not enough men to serve these churches. Moreover, many of the women are stronger leaders. Yet some churches will do without a pastor rather than hire a woman. One of them has stated openly that they will die first, and they are not far from it. They remind me of a comment made by a friend of mine who is a nun. She was talking about the resistance of her church to women priests, and she said that they won't ordain even the most qualified women, but "any old man will do." How true it is—and how sad!

In most student churches, however, the majority of the members can accept women in ministry. Usually there are only a few who will not, and sometimes only one. Because the majority do not want to offend the one, or the few, the church suffers from inadequate leadership. The reason is quite simple—the one or the few do not care about the common good. What they want is more important than what is good for their church. They are cut from the same cloth as the young MBA.

This kind of attitude sometimes dominates churches. Wherever it does is to be found a weak and ineffective church. It is like a body whose parts have no sense of working on behalf of the whole. When church members lose sight of the larger body of which they are a part, the whole body suffers. This is true in congregations, and it is true within denominations. And if we have sufficient ecumenical visions, we know that it is also true for the church universal. Lack of concern for the common good is one of the most subtle and pervasive influences in church life today that limit vision and thwart ministry.

One way churches can help their members learn to work for the common good is to start making decisions in the Quaker tradition of consensus. Votes in a church never result in some people winning and others losing. The real truth is, in the church either everyone wins or every loses. That is the nature of the church. I think it is time we stopped voting on decisions in the church and adopted the harder way of trying to work by consensus decision-making. Decision by consensus requires taking the time to let the Spirit work among church members. It means we have to be patient with one another, and to let the will of the majority become evident through loving exchange. At that point consensus decision-making means those who do not agree with the majority, when the will of the group is clear, practice what is called "stepping aside." This means that person agrees not to stand in the way of the will of the group.

This way of making decisions will certainly take more time than voting will. In the long run, though, the church as one body is strengthened, whereas voting pits one person against another, for which the body as a whole suffers. It is a foolish way of making decisions in the church. It is also the most dominant form of doing so, which may have more to do with the weakness of churches today than many church leaders want to believe. I think decision by vote is a form of the church shooting itself in the foot. It is self-inflicted punishment done in the name of "efficiency." The damage far outweighs getting quicker decisions.

The common good is one of the most important, yet neglected, themes of the New Testament. It is the most practical way we have to show that we really do love each other because we really do belong to Jesus Christ. (See John 13.) It is a witness worthy of the sacrifices involved.

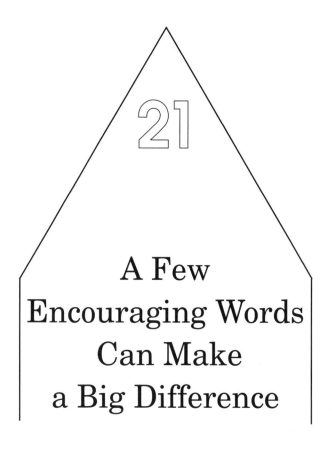

A Few
Encouraging Words
Can Make
a Big Difference

Ministry can sometimes be very discouraging. It's the nature of working with people. Churches are filled with all kinds of people. Whether one is laity or clergy, doing ministry puts one in the position of being criticized. It is true that we cannot please everyone, and that is never more evident than in the church. Critical comments are commonplace. I have felt the sting of criticism many times as a pastor. I have also seen more than a few laity get discouraged to the point of wanting to quit the church because of it.

To some extent criticism goes with the territory when one is a leader. There are always those who think they can do your job better than you can, and they seem to have no hesitation in letting you know. Sometimes the criticism is deserved. Many times it is little more than nitpicking, or making judgments without adequate information. In one church I know, the secretary can always expect a telephone call from one of the members every Monday morning. Something will have been wrong with the Sunday bulletin—a typo or an announcement of a coming event being omitted. Sometimes a bulletin will be left on her desk with mistakes circled in red. She doesn't mind so much that mistakes are pointed out. It is the manner in which it is done that upsets her. Moreover, she says this person never says anything positive when there are no mistakes, or when a job is well done.

That is the problem in the church. It is the preponderance of negative comments in the absence of positive remarks. Many days there are ten negative comments for every positive one. People in leadership hear about their mistakes instantly, but go long periods of time without the slightest word of encouragement. It's not that people have to be patted on the back to do their job. They do it—and usually do it well—without encouragement. But a pat on the back never hurt job performance, and many times it can make more of a difference than most church members realize. The reason is that most church members are unaware of how much criticism their leaders receive. A simple, positive word sometimes makes a church leader's day.

Recently a friend of mine who is a staff member in a large church told me how much an unexpected telephone call from a church member had meant to her. This church has made a lot of changes in its worship service over the last few years. I have attended some of them. I think the worship is a dynamic, exciting experience. Most of the members agree, but the few who don't are the most vocal. The phone call was from a longtime member who told my friend that she wanted her to know how much she and her husband appreciated the new spirit of worship. She described their lives as senior citizens as routine, if not dull. It was exciting, she said, to attend a worship service that combined order with variety and freshness.

That one call made my friend in ministry feel like the work they were doing was worth it after all. That is what a few words of encouragement can do. They lift your spirit and give you strength to go on. We don't do enough of that in the church. Instead we let lay and ministerial leaders hear about all the things they do that people don't like. Any good leader can receive appropriate criticism in the right spirit. But in the absence of encouragement once in a while, criticism can grow old fast. A close friend of mine recently resigned from a very large church to move to a smaller one. He left under the stress of constant criticism. Once he resigned he found out that most people thought that he was doing a good job and appreciated his ministry very much. These people had been the "silent majority" during his tenure at their church. They waited too late to speak. It happens too much in the church. A few encouraging words can make a big difference to someone. That is something every church member should never forget.

Churches
Sometimes
Shoot
the Wounded

A colleague and I sat and listened to the young man talk about his experience of being rejected by his denomination at a time when he and his wife were separated. They had worked through their problems and were now back together. As a student he had worked several summers as a counselor at a church camp. The summer he and his wife separated he had been asked to serve as a supervisor at the same camp. When denominational officials heard about his marital problems, however, they told him his personal situation meant they could not have him on the staff as planned.

He told my friend and me that if there had ever been a time when he needed to be at the camp he knew so well, it was that summer. Instead, his church told him he did not belong. Their decision had hurt him deeply. Describing his pain he said, "You know, it seems like the church is the one institution that shoots the wounded."

What a sad commentary on church life. Churches sometimes do shoot the wounded. People who are experiencing personal pain and struggle feel like the church is the last place they can share it, and for good reason. Church members do not always respond to people in need with compassion and concern. In their concern for morality, church members do not act with wisdom in dealing with people with personal wounds. Divorce, homosexuality, sexual misconduct, alcohol/drug addiction all have been condemned by the church. It is little wonder that people often feel condemned rather than cared for by the church. For some reason church members are ill-equipped to know how to be accepting of persons who are struggling with personal issues and problems.

Consider, for example, the church's response to the AIDS crisis. Recently I was told about a church member who brought a friend with AIDS to his church. As they were standing in line to shake hands with the minister at the close of the service, they overheard someone say, "Well, I certainly hope *he* doesn't come back," speaking, of course, about the man with AIDS. Her comment hurt the man deeply. Thank God it also hurt most of the people standing there.

That is the good side of this. Not all church members shoot the wounded. Sometimes church members contribute to the healing of a life that has been wounded. I personally found this to be the case in my last pastorate. It is not an overstatement to say that I am still in ministry because of the loving support of the elders of that church during a time when I was going through personal struggles. They loved me through the worst time of my life and remained committed to our mutual ministry in the process. I, in fact, resigned at the time, but the elders met in private and voted to reject my resignation. They told me to take sixty days off rather than giving them a sixty-day notice. If, at the end of that time, I still wanted to resign, they would accept my decision. I took a month and came back believing that God was speaking to me through them. I decided to stay in ministry and at that church. Instead of shooting the wounded, they acted with sincere love and support. I shall forever be grateful to them.

The church can do this more than it does. I think we worry too much that we are compromising principles by accepting people who are having problems. We talk about hating the sin, but loving the sinner, as if we are not sinners ourselves. I suspect if all of us would remember that not one of us deserves God's mercy, we might well be more merciful to one another. Not one of us is yet able to cast the first stone at another.

The wounded of this world need to know that church members will be the first ones to welcome them into their fellowship. They should know that the church is the one place where they can go for help and find it. They should know that church members are more interested in giving them a hand or a hug than in making sure they know what sin they have committed. The church needs to build a new reputation in the world that speaks of acceptance more than judgment, healing more than rejection. All of us in the church are, as Father Henri Nouwen has said, "wounded healers." There should never be a time when another "wounded one" is not welcomed. In the church we should never shoot the wounded, for we ourselves are the wounded. Let us never forget it.

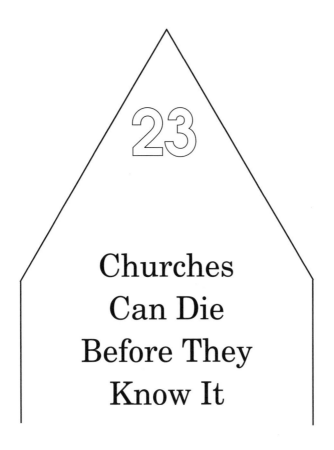

Churches
Can Die
Before They
Know It

The death of a church is a sad thing to see. More churches die than many church members realize. Most of us are acquainted with the struggle of inner city churches to survive. The odds are against them. A few cathedral-type churches have managed to survive the flight to the suburbs. Most, however, have followed their membership out of the central city or disbanded altogether.

My last pastorate was a central city church. We worked long and hard to remain a viable, worshiping congregation. We made progress, and the congregation is still able to support itself, avoiding becoming a mission project for some suburban congregation. When I first went to the church, though, the level of denial regarding the reality of decline was nothing short of astounding. We were "code blue," but nobody wanted to admit it.

A breakthrough came when a colleague in a neighborhood church came to an elders' breakfast to present a paper he had written on the stages of grief of an urban congregation. He was talking about the grief his own church members had experienced as they saw their congregation decline. In a real sense they had waited too late to come to grips with what was happening. When he finished, the first response of one of the elders was that my colleague was talking about our church, not just his own. We were going through the same kind of grief. The others agreed. That was the first time they acknowledged the situation we were facing.

Church members seldom think about their church dying. Even if they see it declining, the idea that one day the doors might actually close just does not register. Any church can die, but most will deny this possibility until it is too late to do anything about it. I suppose denial is only human. Few people think about their own deaths. Other people die; not us. Other people have heart attacks, get cancer, have an accident. We seldom think that such things can ever happen to us.

The same thing happens in churches. Other churches die. Not ours. Other churches reach the point where they cannot pay their bills, cannot afford to hire a minister. Other churches let their buildings deteriorate beyond repair. Many church members think that their church will never die as long as they are alive.

The fact is, churches sometimes die long before the doors close. There are different ways of dying. Elton Trueblood said many years ago that a church can exist long after the Spirit has gone out of it. The church is an institution, but it is more than an institution. Activity does not automatically mean a church is alive. Ezekiel's vision of the Spirit of God leaving the temple and Jerusalem (Ezekiel 10:4) scores this very point. Human activity in a building called a church does not necessarily mean it is a church. That is why it is essential that church members understand to whom the church belongs. The words of the psalmist speak to the church:

> Unless the LORD builds the house,
> those who build it labor in vain.
> Unless the LORD guards the city,
> the guard keeps watch in vain.
>
> Psalm 127:1

The church's life, as underscored earlier, comes from God, not from church members. This means that as church members we have to take care that we do not rely so much upon ourselves that we ignore the power of the Holy Spirit.

In practical terms I think this suggests that whenever churches try to be anything other than the church, they can die before they know it. What was so exciting in my last congregation was the fact that we did not have the luxury of trying to be anything but the church. We were so desperate for the power of God to work in and through us that we could not afford to take things into our own hands.

Once we realized this to be the case, then we also got a better picture of what we needed to be doing. We could not assume business as usual. We could not live in the past. We could hardly keep up with the present, yet we needed to be thinking seriously about the future. It was not a time for wringing hands and weeping and wailing. It was a great opportunity to see, not what we could do, but what God could do in, through, and to us.

Sometimes a church needs to focus attention on its own life. Not that it should ignore mission to others. It is a matter of emphasis at a given time. I think many churches need to spend some time focusing on the quality of their inward life before they put much emphasis on bringing in new members. Dying churches need to heal from the inside out. Otherwise they are treating symptoms while ignoring the disease.

As strange as it may sound, there are worse things that can happen to a church than dying. One of them is what Gordon Cosby, pastor of the famed Church of the Savior in Washington D. C., calls not knowing how to die a clean death. Some institutions hang on, he says, long after their mission has been completed, making a futile attempt to keep alive what has already died. I know some churches like that. They need to die a clean death by celebrating the ministry they have had and then letting it go.

On the other hand, I know some churches that are dying when their time has not come. They have lost vision and commitment. They are doing little more than trying to perpetuate an institution whose life went out of it a long time ago. These are the kinds of churches that die before they know. Some of them die because they don't have enough people left to carry on the ministry. The truth is, however, they probably died before the numbers got so low. They just did not realize what was happening. It is possible that they died without ever knowing if it was a clean death or not.

I believe there will always be the church. The Word needs flesh. But there may not always be my church. It might die. If it does because its ministry is complete, praise be to God! It would be a shame, though, if it died when it did not have to, because its members did not see it coming. It is a sobering thought, but I believe it is true—churches can die before they know it.

Healthy Churches Make Things Happen

"God helps those who help themselves." I've heard that all my life. In fact, as a child I was told this bit of wisdom was in the Bible. Many years passed before I found out it wasn't. Apparently most church members now know this aphorism is not in the Bible. It has been a long time since I heard someone say it was. But I still hear the phrase a lot, usually when someone is trying to make a case against the church helping poor people. They just don't say it's in the Bible, although some of them say it with such passion that you get the impression they think it should be.

I used to be very skeptical of the motives of anyone who said that God helps those who help themselves, especially when they added "only" to the phrase—"God 'only' helps those...." Lately, though, I have begun to admit that there is some "truth" to what they are saying. Not that I believe God only helps those who help themselves, or that God does not help those who do not help themselves. What I think has merit is the fact that God will and does help us all the time, but God will not and does not do for us what we can and must do for ourselves. I do believe God helps us even when we choose not to help ourselves. I also believe that whatever way God does help us, God always leaves undone that which we can and must do ourselves—and for ourselves. This is the only way I can see that God can be a responsible parent. Otherwise the Almighty becomes a party to our foolishness.

Within this context I want to suggest that church members need to realize that a healthy church is one that does what God leaves for its members to do. In other words, human effort counts for something. It counts for a lot, in fact. There is no substitute for it, and no excuse for its absence. Someone once said that there are three kinds of people in the world: People who make things happen; people who let things happen; and people who wonder what happened! We need churches full of the first kind of people—those who make things happen. We have had too many who have let things happen, and now they are wondering what has happened.

I have already said more than you probably wanted to read about our dependence upon God for our life as the church. The very first chapter talked about the church belonging to God and not to us. None of that, however, should be construed to suggest that it is all up to God, that we have no significant role to play in how our lives are played out—either personally or collectively as the church. It borders on blasphemy to use God to excuse our irresponsible actions, or inaction. That is also to take the Lord's name in vain. It is a mistake to think that the church's life depends solely on us, and it is a mistake to think the church can have a life when we contribute nothing to it. That is not the way God works.

For some reason known only to God, divine wisdom has ordained that God use human beings to do heaven's work here on earth. Personally I think a good case could be made that that was one mistake God made, but then who am I to judge the wisdom of God? Its particular merits aside, it is clear that God has chosen to use us in the divine work of saving this planet from human destruction. This can only mean that God expects something from us. We are not here to sit on our hands. There is work to be done, and we are the ones who can and need to do it.

I am quite convinced that the best of human efforts cannot make the church be the church, simply because the church is a divine institution. Nonetheless the church cannot be the church without human beings. There would be no point. It is the human face of Christ, even as Christ was the human face of God. As long as we do not give into the tempter's snare and become arrogant enough to think that the church belongs to us, our efforts have a place, even an important place.

I believe there are too many churches sitting on their hands. That is, there are too many churches that have hardly come close to realizing the great potential they have for ministry in today's world. I think we have a failure of nerve in the church. It takes the form of playing it safe, of never risking anything for the sake of ministry. Passive discipleship is a contradiction in terms. The very nature of belonging to Jesus means we are doers. That is what scripture teaches—be doers of the Word, and not hearers only (James 1:22).

Recently I had a disturbing conversation with a woman who belongs to a church in my own denomination. She devotes much time and money to social concerns in our city. She also holds a leadership position in her church. She told me that she was considering leaving her church, and perhaps our denomination. The reason she gave? We were, in her words, "too vanilla." What she meant was that her minister was more interested in not rocking the boat on important issues than in addressing them openly, and because of his long ministry there, the church had become the same way. She went on to say that she was convinced that this was one of the reasons nonchurch people were not being attracted to the church. Talk about a different perspective. At a time when pollsters have convinced politicians that they should duck every major issue they can because the public doesn't want to deal with them, this woman is convinced that the church that does address issues will attract others to its life and ministry.

I frankly believe she may be right. At the very least it would be a tragedy if her church lost her. She is someone who believes people can and should make things happen in their church. I believe we need more church members who think this way.

Yet the challenge to make things happen in the church is not only a matter of doing good deeds. It also has to do with the inward life of a congregation. It means changing when and where change can give new life. It means responding to a changing world with intention and courage. It means acting instead of simply reacting. A church that makes things happen in its life is a church filled with people whose primary interest is being the church. Such a church will always be on the move, always be ready to take the next—and even a new—step in ministry, always aware that while its power comes from God, its actions must come from its own members. I would love to be a member of such a church!

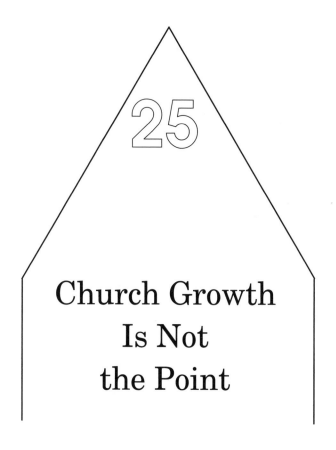

Church Growth
Is Not
the Point

A Presbyterian minister named Robert Hudnut wrote a book by this title years ago. I liked it then. I still think his point is right on target. Church growth is not what the church is all about. I am convinced, in fact, that whenever it does become the point, the gospel is compromised.

I realize that saying this runs contrary to the dominant mood of the church today. In this age of declining memberships, church growth has become very much the point. In my own denomination many churches have added "Church Growth" to their Evangelism Committee name. The argument is that there is nothing wrong with focusing on church growth, that in fact mainline churches have gotten too liberal and that is why they have not focused on growth. The growth of fundamentalist churches is cited as support for this claim.

The truth is, the church as a whole, conservative or liberal, is in decline in North America. Individual churches may be growing, while others are declining. Overall, however, churches are losing ground. Certainly no Christian wants to see this happen, and the reasons for it are much more complex than some church members believe. Several factors have put us where we are. I think the situation should concern us. It may be that we are not proclaiming the gospel in effective and attractive ways.

That does not mean, though, that the church should now make growth its major focus, or a focus at all. The book of Acts says that God added to the church those who were being saved (Acts 2:47). What this means to me is that growth in the church is an act of God, the result of the movement of the Holy Spirit, just as it happened when the church was born. The role of church members is to be faithful covenant partners. Growth is not within the realm of our responsibility. We are not in the business of "church saving," although it sounds as if we should be according to those who are promoting church growth.

We have made growth a sign of faithfulness. This is similar to those who invert the Deuteronomic ethic of blessings and curses. Deuteronomy says that God blesses those who are good and curses those who are not. Some people turn this around, as the friends of Job did, to mean that those who prosper must be blessed by God, or at least be doing something right. According to this way of thinking, growing churches are blessed by God—or doing something right. The implication, though seldom stated outright, is that churches that are not growing are not doing something right, or perhaps not doing anything at all.

The truth is, churches can grow without God having anything to do with it. People like to be entertained, and some growing churches are doing just that—entertaining people. Some of them admit to it without any apology.

They believe the church must learn to compete with the world of secular entertainment in order to grow. Since growth is a goal, entertainment becomes the means to the end.

Some growth occurs simply because a church is located in a growing area. Most growing churches are, which is why few urban churches are experiencing numerical growth. What God has to do with this kind of growth I am not sure. What I do know is that it is quite possible that growth occurs because of social factors that have nothing to do with Christian discipleship.

Some churches are growing by attraction rather than promotion. A friend of mine is the minister of a church like this. In the ten years he has been the pastor, there has been steady growth numerically. More important, the church has grown in its social conscience, which is one of the reasons it is attracting young couples. This kind of growth a church can celebrate because it has not been a goal. It has been a by-product of their ministry.

There is nothing inherently good or bad about church growth. The size of a congregation does not in itself tell anything about its faithfulness. Growth can be encouraging to a church, or it can lead a church into cultural bondage. The point is that strength in the church is not in numbers. I grew up in one of the largest churches in my denomination. We were also a prejudiced, racist, sexist congregation who believed in a God who was white, Protestant, and male. Size said nothing about our faithfulness to the gospel.

Sometimes a church can in fact lose members because it chooses faithfulness over compromise. Had my home church board voted to admit blacks as members, as it should have, there is no doubt that many of the members would have withdrawn. It might even happen today. My concern is not to condemn my home church. It was just like the rest of the churches in my hometown. The point is, size has nothing to do with discipleship.

Discipleship is what really matters in the church. That is the point! Not growth. Living as ambassadors for

Jesus Christ is our calling, regardless of its impact on others. All church members know that if they live the gospel, they will find themselves going against the grain of the dominant culture. That may or may not produce growth.

In the Presbyterian *Book of Common Order* the church is described as "Christ's faithful evangelist." This mission is said to include "making disciples," "demonstrating by the love of its members...and by the quality of its common life the new reality in Christ," and "participating in God's activity in the world...by healing and reconciling and binding up wounds...ministering to the needs of the poor, the sick, the lonely, and the powerless...engaging in the struggle to free people from sin, fear, oppression, hunger and injustice...." Then it says:

> The church is called to undertake this mission even at the risk of losing its life, trusting in God alone as the author and giver of life....

This is why growth is not the point. It never has been. It never should be. Faithfulness is the point. It always has been. It always should be. No matter what it costs. When growth is the point churches sometimes blink at a challenge to pay the cost of living the gospel. If growth occurs because a church does not blink, praise be to God. That is the kind of growth that serves discipleship instead of undercutting it. But growth should never be our aim. Being the church should be. After that, we leave the matter of growth to God.

To some readers this, of course, may sound like the kind of thinking they believe has led the church down the road to decline in the first place. My response is that the decline of any church is never as simple as most of us want to think. We want to be able to identify the problem in simple terms in order to believe there is a simple solution. Neither am I suggesting that growth is a bad thing or that we should not want to grow and, therefore, should go out of our way to be unfriendly to ensure that we don't.

What I am suggesting is that discipleship needs to be our goal, not membership growth. Commitment can attract people into the life of the church. Expecting commitment from them will not turn them away. Making church membership so easy that people fall over the threshold is not the way to build up the life of any congregation. I suppose it is naive, but I am convinced that when churches focus on faithfulness to the gospel, growth takes care of itself.

Ministers Can't Fix Churches

I often hear church members say that if they could get a good minister, their church would turn around. They are saying two things: They believe their church is going in the wrong direction, and they believe a new minister can fix what is wrong. They might be right on the first count, but they are wrong on the second. Ministers can't fix churches.

This is not to say that ministers cannot make a difference in a church's life. They can make matters worse, and they can help improve a bad situation. Churches need good leaders, and good leaders make a big difference in a church's life. But even the best leader cannot fix a church that has problems. Ministry does not work that way because people don't work that way. People are the source of the problems in the churches, and no one can "fix" people.

When a church experiences numerical decline, or when disgruntled members show their feelings by withdrawing, church members begin to think that what they need is new leadership who can lead them out of these problems. This kind of thinking is similar to people believing that if they move to a new job or a new city life will be better. Chances are they will feel better for a while, but it will not take long before they realize that the move did not produce the results they thought it would.

"Fixes" do not come that easy. Churches decline for many reasons, and decline itself comes in different forms. Ministers can be tempted into believing they can "fix" such churches, that they are the answer to a church's problems. My experience is that ministers who think this way are the ones who inevitably make a bad situation worse. The reason is that this kind of thinking focuses on externals, when the real problem is a spiritual one. Troubled churches have a troubled spirit. The way they can experience renewal is to recognize that they need to do the hard work of spiritual formation and development.

Churches that look to a minister to "fix" them, though they would never use those words, are making an impossible demand. The burden of the church's life falls to the minister, and she becomes the one to whom church members look for solutions to the problems they face. That is a recipe for disaster. Even if the situation improves initially, it is usually temporary. Sometimes a minister manages to keep the lid on the problems, but they resurface once he leaves. In the meantime, ministers often pay a high price in stress for trying to live up to the expectations of church members who want them to "fix" their church.

Ministers can do many things, but the one thing they cannot do is to "fix" a church. Those who expect them to, and those who want to do it, are dealing with symptoms rather than the disease. Their understanding of the role of the ordained and the laity, their concept of church and ministry, even the depth of their spiritual life, are far from adequate to sustain them in ministry. Laity who expect their minister to "fix" their church, and ministers who want to be "fixers," are victims of one of the most serious and at the same time subtle temptations of ministry—which is to look for a "savior" in the wrong place and in the wrong person.

I wish ministers could "fix" churches. It would make church life a lot easier. Ministers could function like medical doctors—make the right diagnosis and then prescribe the needed remedy. As long as the "patient" (church) did what the "doctor" (minister) ordered, it would get better.

That, of course, is a fantasy, and not a good one at that. Problems are part of living because living has to do with people trying to find meaning and purpose in their lives. Wrestling with problems is a part of growing and maturing, not only emotionally and psychologically, but also spiritually. I think Aldous Huxley was correct when he pictured utopian existence in his novel *Brave New World* as dull and boring, without meaning because no challenges remained, all problems had been solved.

Problems are not the problem in a church. The real problem is when church members look to a minister to solve all their church's problems, instead of realizing church problems of any kind never yield themselves to simple solutions. Easy answers seldom "fix" anything, and never last beyond the life of a bandage.

On the other hand, church members joining together to work on problems can itself be a source for renewed life in a church. When lay people and the ministerial leadership recognize that there are no easy solutions to the problems they face, but that together they can have a significant ministry working on them, a new spirit will be sensed. That church will have vision and direction.

Ministers can help churches that have problems. But ministers are not "messiahs." Which means they can not—and should not ever try to—"fix" a church.

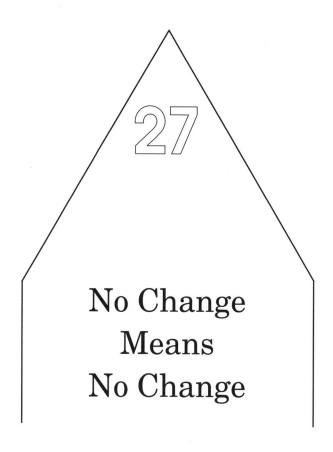

No Change
Means
No Change

Somewhere I have heard it said that doing the same things the same way they've always been done never produces different results. Every church member should know this already, but it seems to be something they often forget. That is why change is so difficult for them. Churches spin their wheels doing what they've been doing the same way they've always done it, and then they are surprised when things turn out the same way they've always been. They become discouraged because nothing is different. They feel like they work hard at getting nowhere. The problem is that instead of recognizing what they are doing, they decide to give up the hope of things changing for the better. Their spirits sag and the wind goes out of their sails.

I was a supply preacher once in a church that was going down. The membership was getting old, the building was in need of repair, membership was static, and finances were getting tighter. They were sure that the right minister could turn things around. Finally they called a very capable man in his late thirties. It seemed to be a good match. The church was excited about his coming.

I visited with him from time to time over a period of a year. He was going through the typical "honeymoon" period, but I could tell that he was not feeling very good about the move he had made. Into his second year we had occasion to talk at length during a conference we were both attending. He was discouraged, even angry, convinced that this move had been a big mistake. He said that when he first arrived he could sense that most of the members were ready for something new. Enthusiasm was high and participation had increased during the first year rather significantly. Attendance was up 20 percent over the previous five years. Offerings had increased as well.

His concern was that it seemed the ministry had hit a plateau and was no longer moving ahead. He was feeling an inward pressure to try some new programs to get things moving again. He was discouraged because he felt like the old leadership was fighting him every step of the way. They were glad for the new spirit in the church, but they did not want to venture beyond the known and tried ways of the past. They seemed to be convinced that all they had to do was to do what they had been doing all their lives and things would continue to go up. They refused to believe that doing this would eventually lead them back to where they had been for the last ten years.

New life cannot be sustained by doing the same things the same way they have always been done. Inevitably this leads to the same things that have always been. Sometimes it does not even produce the old results. Church members seem surprised when this happens. Yet it is as predictable as a farmer planting crops the same way they have always been planted. The best he can hope for is what he has always gotten. At worst he won't even get that.

At the same time there is a law of nature church members need to remember. It is that whatever does not learn to adapt to changing conditions dies. That is why there are no dinosaurs. The capacity to adapt determines the future of any kind of life. Institutions are no different. Businesses that do not adapt to today's market go out of business. Colleges and seminaries that do not adapt to changing conditions decline and close their doors.

The church is an institution that also has to adapt to changing conditions. It is not exempt from this law of nature. Churches that refuse to change, that want to keep things the way they have always been, are churches that have no chance to meet the needs of today's world. They are "dinosaur" churches that want to survive, but refuse to do what is necessary to adapt to the environment in which they find themselves.

The way we do anything will serve us for a while, but almost always a new way is needed at some point to produce different, and, sometimes, better results. There is, of course, no guarantee that new life will be experienced. But it is for sure that doing ministry the same way it has always been done will at best produce what always has been. It is a paradox, but in a world of constant change, no change means no change.

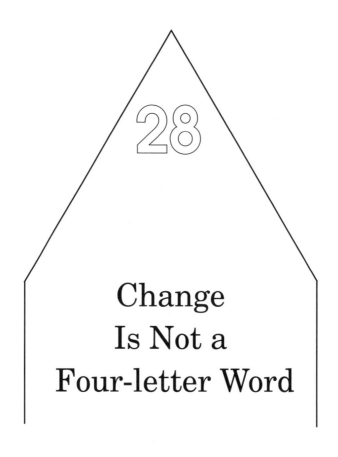

Change
Is Not a
Four-letter Word

Change is so traumatic for some church members
that they respond to the word itself as if it were of the
four-letter variety. Such people believe in tradition. Tradition is what church means to them. They may not
realize it, but for them the church is the last bastion of
resistance to modernity. The late French archbishop,
Marcel Lefebvre, once remarked that the church's future
lies in its past. That is the way people think who believe
change is a four-letter word.

I believe tradition has its place. I am not ready to
throw out old ways for something new just because it is
new. Tradition is what gives us identity and stability.
That is why Tevye of *Fiddler on the Roof* insists on his

children following traditional roles. He fears they will lose who they are if they reject tradition.

Tevye's fears, however, rest on the mistaken notion that tradition and change cannot co-exist. Such people believe change erodes tradition. In the story of Israel, on the other hand, we find a different point of view. The element of adaptation becomes a critical factor in the preservation of the traditions of Israel. The people of Israel preserved their identities and lifestyles by learning how to adapt their traditions to changing circumstances. We know, for example, that in the oldest recitals of the story of Israel, the conquest of the land was a part of it:

> The LORD brought us out of Egypt with a mighty hand and an outstretched arm, with a terrifying display of power, and with signs and wonders; and he brought us into this place and gave us this land, a land flowing with milk and honey.
>
> Deuteronomy 26:8–9

Yet when the Torah (the first five books of the Bible) was later put together, the story of the conquest was not included. The reason was obvious. They were no longer rulers of the land their ancestors conquered, and would not be again until the establishment of the modern state of Israel. Nonetheless the land continued to be a part of the story that gave the Jews their sense of identity. Moreover, the people learned how to be a people of faith without the temple that was twice destroyed. The survival of the Jews is the story of a people who learned how to adapt their traditions to changing circumstances. It is a lesson Christians need to learn.

There is a basic law of nature: that which does not learn to adapt to changing conditions dies. There are no exceptions. What survives adapts because change is the primary constant in life. We can run from change. We can resist it. We can curse it. It will not go away. It goes to bed with us and rises with us in the morning. The chemical/physical changes our bodies go through every day are reminders of the constancy and inevitability of change in all of life. Nothing can stop it. Nothing can avoid it—including the church.

It puzzles me why church members do not understand this law of nature. Their resistance to change is precisely the way to lose the very traditions they want to preserve. While bemoaning the loss of members and the graying of their church, these people continue to resist efforts to change the life of their church. They do not understand one simple fact of life—doing things the same way they've always been done never produces different results.

In my last pastorate the elders became a different group, truly committed and able to care for the spiritual life of the church, when they finally made some changes in the way they conducted their meetings. The need for change finally hit home when one man whose family had been in the church for many years told the group that he did not have time in his schedule to come to an elders' meeting when, in his opinion, it was a waste of time. Besides, he went on to say, he believed the way the meetings were being conducted prevented them from learning how to do what they were supposed to do in the first place—provide spiritual leadership to the congregation.

That night was the beginning of a transformation in that group of church elders. They started coming to grips with the reality of a new day where their position in the church was different than it had been. What they discovered, to their surprise and joy, was that learning to adapt to changing circumstances was the means whereby they preserved their role in the life of the church. A new respect for them developed among the members. Instead of being viewed as those who opposed every new idea that was suggested, they began to be respected as leaders trying to lead the church into the future.

Change is not easy for anyone. My two young-adult children have been making me feel the dis-ease of accepting change for a long time. They just do not think about things the way I do, and there is not one thing I can do about it. I could try to pull them back into my world, but I know it would not work. Every parent is tempted to do that, and most of the time we have the good sense to realize we cannot. It is not easy. But we have to accept the fact that their world is different from ours, or we lose them completely.

What is true in our families is also true in the church. The Bible does not say that the church is the same yesterday, today, and forever. That is what it says about Christ (Hebrews 13:8). Some church members seem to have the two confused. Not only is the church not the same yesterday, today, and forever, it cannot be. The church must adapt to the age in which it finds itself if it wants to play a significant role in people's lives.

I think we make accepting change harder than it has to be by confusing substance and form. The substance of the church's life is Christ. It is our faith that in Christ God was reconciling the world to the divine will (2 Corinthians 5:19). Our first commitment is to belong to Christ before we belong to anything or anyone else. Then it becomes our responsibility to engage in acts of compassion in the name of Jesus Christ. This is the substance of our faith. The form of this substance is the way we organize and function as a community of believers. The form is the body; the substance is the message. Each is important, but the form can change without losing the substance of what we are about. The form is the means to an end. The substance is the end.

Change is not a four-letter word. It is not something to be resisted or feared or fought. We do have to give careful thought to change. Form has its place. But change is ever-present. The world we live in today is not the same world our parents lived in, or we grew up in. It is certainly not the same world in which Jesus lived. More changes have taken place in the last fifty years than all the combined changes of previous history. It is naive to think the church can function the way it always has and still be relevant to the modern age. The tradition has to be adapted to be relevant.

But change in the church is necessary for reasons far less grand than the flow of history. Change in the church is a necessity whenever new leadership emerges. No two people think or do things in the same way. One way is not always better than another, just different. George Brett and Wade Boggs have very different styles of swinging a baseball bat. Both of them are great hitters. To try to get Brett to swing like Boggs would ruin his hitting skills, and vice versa. They are different people and have different styles.

Change comes because people have different styles, different ideas, different tastes. Leadership changes in a church mean having different people with different styles. A new leader may want to do something in a way different from the previous one, or try something that has never been tried. That is the nature of being human. That is why changes are suggested. It is part of being different people. The only way never to have change in a church is never to have anyone new in leadership. Some churches operate this way. Most of the churches like this that I know of died a long time ago. They just don't know it.

There is nothing more important for church members than to learn how to cope with change in a creative and open way. The well-being of any church depends on it. Rather than saving tradition, resistance to change undercuts ministry and usually ends up dividing churches. At the very least it causes those who want change to lose heart and give up on the church. The fact that change is hard for us does not mean that we always have to resist it. I know a woman whose first response to any new idea is to be against it. Her minister knows that every time he suggests anything new she will be the first to oppose it. Apparently she has forgotten that everything old once was new. The older I get the more it seems true that the more things change the more they stay the same. But it is only in trying to cope with change that we find this out. We also find out that change is not as bad as we thought it was. It is certainly not a four-letter word.

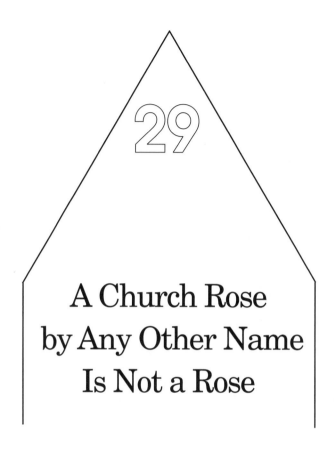

A Church Rose
by Any Other Name
Is Not a Rose

"A rose by any other name is still a rose." This well-known aphorism speaks of a basic truth about life that is reassuring. Some things remain. Some things are permanent. At the same time, though, this statement suggests that names do not matter, that things are what they are no matter what they are called. This may be true for a rose, or other things, but it is not true for all things. It is certainly not true for a "church rose." In the church names matter. They matter a lot. What we call something influences what that something is. In other words, names reflect and shape identity.

They did in the Bible. Abram became Abraham. Sarai became Sarah. Jacob became Israel. Simon became Peter. Saul became Paul. In the Bible names matter. This is because the ancients believed names held something of the essence of the person or thing they represented. That is why Jews even to this day do not speak the name of God. When a reader comes to the name Yahweh, the word *Adonai* is substituted. The true name of God holds within it the holiness of God. To speak God's name is to violate that holiness.

I believe names matter in the church. Words shape who we are, and who we are determines what we do. The words we use in the church not only reveal what we think, but make a difference in the way we think and act. What we call ourselves—and what we do—is often how we think of ourselves and what we become. Words are not neutral. They have power to shape and influence the identity and mission of the church.

Let me illustrate this point. Most of the churches I know are organized by committees. Everything from evangelism to stewardship to education is done by committee. Sometimes these groups are called departments, or even task forces. Yet what we are about in the church is ministry. It is a puzzle to me that we do not call what we do by its name—ministry. In my last pastorate we stopped using the name "committee" for our work and started calling it ministry. It made a significant difference in the way the members thought about themselves. To serve in a ministry had a very different meaning to them than did serving on a committee. Serving in a ministry reflects a call to commitment, and, at the same time, helps to create it. Serving on a committee does not. There is nothing people dread more than serving on a committee. Usually we have to convince them that we don't expect much from them to get them to agree to serve, which undercuts the very work we want them to be involved in.

The church is about ministry. Using the name, instead of calling what we do a committee or department or task force, changes the way church members think about their role in the church. In our church we even stopped asking people to serve directly. Instead we asked them to volunteer. We took the risk that no one would. They did. And when they did they knew they were accepting responsibility for the quality of that group's life and ministry. It changed the way we thought and acted as church members.

Changing names had the same effect on the elders to whom I referred previously. They had not always been the "pastoring" group they are now. For years they had called themselves "the board of elders." That is precisely how they thought of themselves—as a board. Their primary function, however, was to nurture the spiritual life of the congregation. But their meetings were conducted like a board meeting. No time was spent preparing themselves for their true ministry. Besides, they no longer had the power to govern the church that they once had. The structure had been changed so that the real power was in the hands of the general board of the church, which was representative of a broader spectrum of the church membership. Nevertheless, the elders would meet monthly to act as if they were a power-brokering group in the church.

Once we made the decision to stop calling ourselves a "board," we began to think of ourselves in a different way. We agreed to structure the meetings to equip us to do what we were supposed to do—be spiritual leaders in the church. The group's life changed dramatically. They became the spiritual leaders who led our church to a new understanding of itself and its ministry through some very difficult times.

It sounds too simple, of course, but it all began with a change in name. Names matter in the church. What we call ourselves is how we think of ourselves, and how we think of ourselves determines what we do. Earlier I said that the church is not a business. The problem is that we think of ourselves that way because we have organized ourselves like a business, and, thus, we use business language to describe what we do. Church members serve on committees and boards, so that is how they think about their church membership.

I think Jesus would be shocked at this kind of language. He never called anyone to serve on a committee or board. He called—and calls—people to discipleship. To respond to this invitation is to respond to a call to ministry. That is what we are about. I think that is the name we should be using for what we do.

One implication in all the above is something very important: structure is not neutral! How we organize ourselves influences what we do. Too many church members fail to recognize the power of structure to determine our life together. Jesus said that new wine should not be put into old wineskins, nor should a new patch be sewn on old cloth (Matthew 9:16–17). The institution of the church—its structure—has played no small role in creating the problems churches today face. From the relationship of the ordained and laity to the way church members think about their responsibilities in the church, structure has been a major factor—a negative one in my opinion.

The structure in most churches serves primarily to perpetuate the institution, but does little to encourage and nurture church members in accepting responsibility in ministry. It does little to lead them into the joy of ministry. I think church structure has in fact become stifling to people. We have counted on "spirit" to keep people excited and involved, and discounted the fact that the "structure" kills the spirit. I have seen more than a few people return from a spiritual retreat renewed and excited, only to find all the spirit gone out of them six months later. The reason was that there was nothing in the structure of their church to nurture the renewed life they had experienced. They went back to the same old things, and ended up feeling the same old way.

Structure is not neutral, any more than names do not matter. The way a church is organized will enhance or hinder that church's ministry. Structure makes a difference. Names make a difference. What we call ourselves and how we do what we are called to do either contribute to or stand in the way of our being the church of Jesus Christ on earth. A rose by any other name is still a rose, except in the church. There a name makes a great deal of difference.

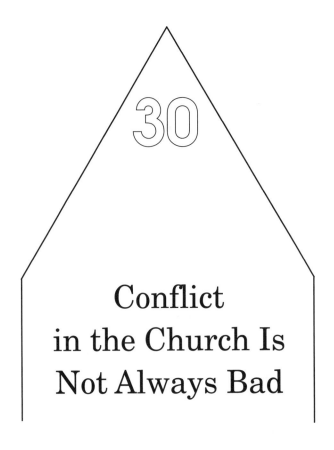

Conflict
in the Church Is
Not Always Bad

A sermon I heard years ago was entitled, "Learning How to fight like Christians in the Church." I don't even remember now who preached it. I do remember the sermon, though. It challenged the attitude in the church that conflict in a church is always bad. Most of the members I know believe conflict in the church is a terrible thing and should be avoided at all costs. So far as I can tell this attitude has never managed to eliminate conflict. It has only managed to keep people from confronting it directly. Death and taxes are supposed to be the only sure things in life. My experience is that conflict is another one. The only way conflict can be avoided is for everyone to live and work alone. Churches are filled with people who talk about how we should love one another, which for them means always getting along and never having any trouble. This kind of attitude is naive concerning human relations. It can also lead to serious problems by its resistance to confronting conflict openly.

Churches have conflict because church members are people. Even Jesus' disciples had conflict. Once as they traveled with Jesus on the way to Capernaum they got into an argument over who was the greatest among them (Mark 9:33–34). Being in the presence of Jesus himself did not keep them from having conflict. Conflict in the church has a long history.

Conflict in a church can be bad. When it goes on all the time it creates an atmosphere of tension that undercuts any ministry of spiritual growth and nurture. I believe churches have personalities. Some churches have a contentious personality, just as some people do. They are unhappy with themselves, which leads them to fuss and fight about everything, most of which is, as a friend of mine characterizes it, of "monumental insignificance." This is unhealthy for the members, and it is very discouraging to any visitors to such a church. Most of the time they don't come back.

On the other hand, conflict that has to do with discerning and doing the will of God can be healthy and constructive. There is some truth to the notion that some things are worth fighting for. In the church this translates into being willing to confront important questions forthrightly, and to speak one's convictions. One of my favorite verses of scripture is 1 Peter 3:15–16b: "Always be ready to make your defense to anyone who demands from you an accounting for the hope that is in you; yet do it with gentleness and reverence." There is a place for standing up for what one believes if it is done in humility and respect for others.

One of the most frustrating experiences a church leader can have is to be in a meeting where she knows people are not speaking up, yet disagree with the decisions being made. Many of these same people will express their opinions out on the parking lot, but they refuse to speak in a meeting. Sometimes they do not speak up because they are intimidated by others in a meeting. This is understandable. Sometimes, though, it is because they do not want to create conflict. They think it is better to say nothing than to express a different view and get into conflict with someone. Besides, they don't want to hurt anyone's feelings.

I know very few people who like conflict. I know people who like it less than others. Most people would be happy without conflict in their lives. But it is a fact of life, and the question church members face is how are they going to deal with it. Churches suffer more from failing to confront a conflict than they would if they dealt with it. If we remember to speak with gentleness and reverence, we can speak forthrightly in the firm trust that God will be at work among us to bind up wounds and heal hurt feelings.

This, I think, is the real issue: where is God in the midst of church conflicts? I once heard a colleague who teaches pastoral care at another seminary say that when churches avoid conflict, they are witnessing to the fact that they believe alienation is stronger than forgiveness. I believe she is right. That is why there are worse things than conflict in a church. One is when we believe our church cannot deal with conflict and remain the church. The foundation of the gospel is forgiveness—divine and human. When church members know themselves to be the community of the forgiven, they are able to confront conflict without fear. They do not confront it alone. They confront it as the body of Christ where the redemptive work of God's Spirit is always at work.

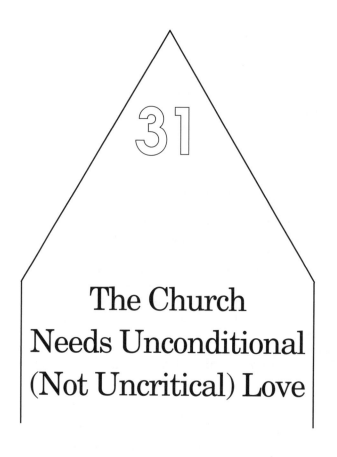

The Church
Needs Unconditional
(Not Uncritical) Love

I used to think that I could have a love/hate relationship with the church. A lot of Christians feel this way. Theologian Paul Tillich once remarked that the church he loved so much was also the source of his greatest frustrations. Anyone who has been in the church very long, especially in a leadership role—lay or clergy—knows why Tillich made this comment. The church can give life, and it also seems to be able to take it away.

The problem I found in thinking this way is that a love/hate attitude toward the church easily becomes a "take it or leave it" attitude. The threat of breaking fellowship is the natural child of the union of these two attitudes. That has been the cause of more than a few people quitting a particular church, and the cause of just as many church splits. When people threaten to break fellowship in the midst of a discussion or disagreement, the whole agenda changes. Dialogue is no longer possible. Even worse, trust breaks down. When a church member can take or leave their commitment to their church, then it is difficult to trust that they want what is best for the church. Perhaps I am being overly optimistic about human nature, but I believe it is possible to love the church unconditionally, while maintaining a critical attitude about her faults. If more of us did, there would be fewer church splits.

Unconditional love for the church is not an ideal that has no place in the real world. If we love Jesus Christ even a little, then we can love the church enough not to threaten to withdraw if we do not get our way. This is not to suggest that church members should never leave a church and go somewhere else. It means that this should always be the last resort, be done prayerfully, and be done without any intention of creating problems for the church they are leaving. There are appropriate ways to leave a church, and we will find them, if we truly love the church.

Neither does it mean that we cannot be critical of the church of which we are a part. That is why I suggested at the beginning that unconditional love does not mean uncritical. Criticism and love can work together. Criticism rooted in love will be constructive because its intention is to help. The absence of love means the intention to help is missing. When it is, nothing constructive can come from it.

There once existed such a thing as church loyalty. Members would stay in their church, working in it and through it, no matter what was going on. They were determined to be loyal. They had a larger vision of the church than any particular moment or situation. They were unwilling to let anything or anyone cause them to leave their church.

All of that was written in the past tense because I am not sure this kind of loyalty exists anymore. Some older members of the churches I have served still have it, but they are in the minority. The vast majority of church members I know and hear about do not have the kind of loyalty that once existed. Today's church members seem to be dominated by a "take it or leave it" attitude. Stick-to-itiveness seems to be in short supply. If they do not get what they want or need, then they go somewhere else. This sounds reasonable, except for the fact that no church will always meet all my wants or needs, or anyone else's. Unless my church can count on me when it does not meet my needs, it is not going to be able to count on me for much of anything in the long run.

The ordained and lay members of any church must be willing to stick with each other because of their love for the church, even when they don't care much for each other, if there is to be any real ministry taking place. That may sound strange. After all, what is the church except the people who are supposed to love each other? I suggest the church is more than the people. It is first and foremost Jesus Christ. If I belong to him first, then there is a good chance that I can learn how to love the church in spite of not getting along with everyone, or in spite of problems that might drive me insane.

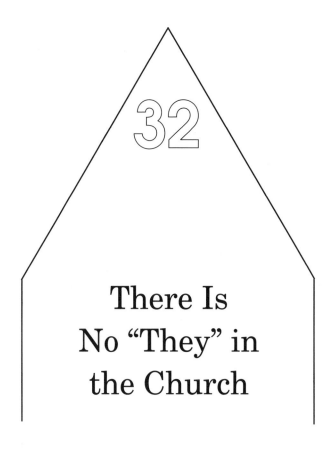

There Is No "They" in the Church

For years now I have been hearing about a group of people in the church that I want to get to know. These people are in every church. Their name is "they." Perhaps you know them. "They" are church members other church members talk about all the time. Because of the way "they" are talked about, I am convinced these are people of considerable power and influence in the church. I often hear them referred to in this way: "Those people at the church I belong to, 'they' do what 'they' want to. 'They' certainly don't care what the rest of us think."

I think it is amazing how much "they" are talked about. Sometimes I find the conversation very confusing, in the tradition of "Who's on First." In fact, talk about "they" makes about as much sense to me as "Who's on First." "They" are referred to as if "they" are real, live people who are making decisions and doing things that affect other people's lives. It is disturbing just how real mythical figures can become because the more real "they" become to church members, the more damaging their mythical existence can be. "They" are usually blamed for all manner of sin and evil, all kinds of problems in the church. Worst of all, the persistence of the talk about "them" often divides church members into groups of "us" and "them." I suppose that this is what the people who talk about "they" want to happen.

Years ago I was walking through a county flea market when I heard a man and woman talking about building a log cabin. I was thinking about building one myself, which I later did, so I stopped to listen. I heard him ask the woman if the logs were precut. She said yes. He asked if they had been delivered. Again she replied yes. He then asked, "When are they going to start building?" She gave a rather guttural laugh and replied, "They? Jim, 'they' is 'us'!"

That is a word needed in the church. "They" is "us." We—all of us—are the church. I believe most church members actually know this to be the case. Lines separating "they" from "us," for whatever reason, are inappropriate and violate the nature of the church as the body of Christ. The mythical "they" in the church are the people who are willing to give their time and energy to their church. On the whole these kind of people do not seek power or influence. They love their church and want to work on its behalf. Many of them do a lot more than anyone ever knows or even notices. They do not want thanks or praise. They simply want to serve God.

This is not to say that some church members do not enjoy power or relish being able to make decisions. I have known a few in my time. I suppose that almost every denomination has had its version of "ruling elders," a small group of people who use leadership positions in the church to exercise power over the church. But such people are few in number. And many times they hold positions because no one else will take responsibility. This was the case in a very large church in my own denomination where the same man served as chair of the official board for twenty-five years. To a large extent his leadership continued because no one was willing to give the amount of time and energy the position required.

My years of pastoring congregations have convinced me that whatever reality the "they" in churches have is rooted in the apathy of the rest of the members who will not serve in leadership and, therefore, cannot challenge the "they." Indeed, I found it much more difficult to deal with apathetic members than those who wanted to use leadership as power. I have previously mentioned the need for change we faced in the last congregation I served. More than once we would face a crucial decision at a meeting of the official board, only to have those who said they supported change miss the meeting. Later I would hear them fussing about the decision "they" made at the last board meeting. I wanted to scream!

What a difference it might make in congregational life if every member recognized the simple truth that there is no "they" in the church. There is only "us." Moreover, it takes all of "us" to build a vital church. It cannot be done by a few. It cannot be done by more than a few. It requires the best efforts and best attitudes of all of "us."

It's OK
to Have Fun
in Church

The equivalent biblical word for *fun* is *joy*. Jesus said that he had come that we might be filled with joy:

> I have said these things to you so that my joy may be in you, and that your joy may be complete.
>
> John 15:11

Fun in the church is joy, a spirit of enjoying one another and being glad to be together. Fun can be prayerful and it can be dancing. Fun is rejoicing in God's grace and presence. It is praise and thanksgiving. Fun is knowing that no matter what is wrong in our lives, in the church, or in the world, God still is God, and we are being held in divine love. That it is OK to have fun in church is something I believe clergy and laity alike need to appreciate more.

People are attracted to places where they have fun. Ball games, parties, recreation, swimming, skiing. People not only want to have fun; people need to have fun. Life is overbearing when we have no fun. Too often we in the church want to believe that people are out having fun because their lives are empty. It may be true that many people's lives are empty, but having fun is not a way to hide from life. It is a way to live life, enjoy it, even be thankful for it. More than anything else, it may be that we want to believe people are having fun to hide from the emptiness they feel in order to hide the frustration we feel because many of these same people ignore the church.

I believe something is wrong with the spirit in the church these days. It is too "heavy," for lack of a better way of putting it. We seem to be taking ourselves too seriously. It seems our focus on the problems of the world— and there are many—has killed our own spirit of fun and joy. It's as if we feel guilty if we have a little fun in church, as if we are betraying our concern for those who are suffering and need our help. Almost all the pictures of Jesus we see depict him as somber and serious. Perhaps that is the way Jesus was. But I happen to believe that he wasn't. His attendance at the wedding feast in Cana of Galilee (John 2:1–11) at the very least suggests the possibility that Jesus knew how to have a good time, especially when he was willing to solve the problem for the host who discovered he did not have enough wine to serve his guests.

Early on, church leaders convinced the masses that worship was somber and serious. Heavy emphasis was placed on the sin and depravity of humankind. Worshipers were told they were a blot on the creation of God, born in sin and destined to perish in the fires of hell unless they repented and lived a holy and devout life, which, of course, meant supporting the church as it grew wealthier and wealthier. It was during the early centuries of church life that the roots of puritanical religiosity were sown deep. Christianity became a burden to be borne, rather than a joy to be celebrated. I do not believe the church has ever recovered from its early association with somberness. Early American Puritans even attempted to institutionalize the severity of Christian living. Indeed, Puritanism has been defined as the haunting suspicion that somewhere, someone is having fun!

The problem we are discussing is, of course, a theological one. That is, the church has become a house of long faces because of what it believes. And I think Matthew Fox, a Dominican priest, is quite right when he says in his book, *Original Blessing*, that the church has let St. Augustine's doctrine of original sin overshadow the Bible's proclamation of original blessing. Fox argues that the Fall/Redemption way of thinking about the human condition ignores the fact that according to scripture "the universe itself is blessed and graced," and that before anything like original sin there was original blessing.

I think Fox makes an important contribution to western Christianity's understanding of life in the fact that he seeks to bring some balance to the church's theology. Scripture does say that God looked at creation and declared it to be good (Genesis 1:25). My Old Testament colleagues tell me that the Creation story in Genesis 1 carries the notion of God delighting in creation. It is as if God looked upon creation and said, "Wow!"

Sin does not negate this original blessing on creation. Life is a blessing! It is to be enjoyed. If that means anything to us, it means that we can delight in living. One can have fun and be a Christian. Indeed, if there is any place where the goodness of life needs to be the focus, it is in the church. The church should be a community of fun, of joy, of excitement, of delighting in creation. People should not have to wait until church is over to have some fun. They should have fun in church.

That church life can be fun simply means church members can affirm the goodness and blessing of living, even in the face of hardship and pain, death and destruction. We can be serious about social evils and at the same time sing and dance praises to God the Creator. In the words of a familiar song:

Dance, dance, wherever you may be,
I am the Lord of the Dance, said he;
And I'll lead you all, wherever you may be,
And I'll lead you all in the dance, said he.

The Lord of the church is the Lord of the dance! He is the Lord of all life. In the midst of whatever else may be happening to us, we should remember that life itself has been blessed by God at Creation. Thus, life can be full of joy and hope, if we look for them. Life is to be enjoyed and celebrated.

Practically, what this means in the life of a church is that there is an important place for fellowship. Among the things church members do, we need to be together just for the sake of being with one another. When I was young in ministry I thought the world's problems were so demanding that we didn't have time for fellowship in the church. I didn't even like the word *fellowship*. At that early point in my ministry, taking time just for fellowship sounded selfish. What I now know is that fellowship is one way we can have fun with each other in church, and I believe we need that today as much as anything else we do.

My first year in my last pastorate was the church's centennial year. Before I arrived the anniversary committee had planned a Sunday evening fellowship time to be held once a month until the month we celebrated the church's founding. It was a time of fun and games. We came together and played. By the time the anniversary weekend arrived, we were filled with the joy of being with one another. It was a great time in the life of the church. I remember those fellowship evenings with much gratitude.

It really is OK to have fun in the church. It is one way—not the only way—but one way we can thank the God of grace and love for giving us to each other in the church. We don't have to wait for Sunday worship to be over before we can have fun. Jesus came that we might have joy. It's time we loosened up a bit and did more singing and dancing before the Lord—of the church and the Dance.

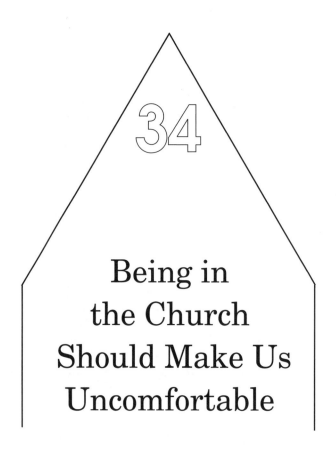

Being in
the Church
Should Make Us
Uncomfortable

A lot is said today about the need for the church to meet the needs of people. Its failure to do so is thought by many people to be the main reason churches are declining in membership. Churches that are growing are thought to be those that are meeting people's needs. And there is reason to believe this is often the case. Most people join the church they believe can best meet their personal needs. It is only logical that they would drop out and go elsewhere when they feel like it no longer does.

It's hard to argue against the importance of the church trying to meet the needs of people. The church, after all, *is* people. I would not join a church that I did not believe could meet my needs. I would not join a church in which I felt uncomfortable or that had a ministry whose focus had little to do with what I thought was important or that had a spirit about it that did not welcome me. It is true, of course, that the desire to have my needs met can go to the extreme where I make church membership into a kind of "consumer's market" proposition. That is, I can want the church to meet my needs so much that my attitude about joining is no different from the way I think about buying a car—I try to get what I want. The fact is, this attitude is fairly common these days. For many people joining a church is like shopping—they look and compare until they find what they consider to be the best deal; that is, the one that has the most to offer them.

I may be highlighting the extreme in regard to the way people think about church membership, but it is also becoming more and more common. As a result, many churches are trying to compete for these people's attention by offering them everything they've ever wanted in a church—and more. A symbol of this situation is the fact that some people are no longer calling their church a "church." Nowadays churches are often called "Christian centers," which means they offer everything from recreation to education. The whole family has a wide variety of activities from which to choose. Again, this kind of effort is not all bad. There is a need for the church to touch the lives of its members in every way it can. This is especially appealing to parents who are concerned about the places and activities their children are invited to outside the church.

At the same time this trend is not altogether good. The emphasis on the church meeting the needs of people, and the subsequent "consumer's market" mentality, has led many churches into serious neglect of the prophetic dimension of their ministry. As churches feel the pressure to "compete" for new members and hold on to those they have, they tend not to want to do anything that would disturb or make people feel uncomfortable. Yet there is an inevitable discomfort all of us in the church should feel when we hear the prophetic word from scripture. It was to the people of God that the prophets spoke in the first place. It is to us that their words still speak.

The reason this is so is because prophetic texts universally call the church back to faithfulness to God. The biblical prophets called upon God's people to confess their sins of idolatry and return to their covenant responsibilities. The context of prophetic speech was the community of God's covenant people. It is still true. Prophetic utterance today is to be heard within the community of God's covenant people, among whom Christians are to be counted. It is because we belong to God and at the same time forsake God that we need to hear the words of the prophets of scripture, including Jesus, who also stood in the prophetic tradition.

Elsewhere I have argued that the American church is enculturated (*Christians Must Choose*, Chalice Press), by which I mean that the church is living more by the values of culture than by the teachings of Jesus. That many churches are "buying" into the consumer mentality of people church-shopping is a telling example of precisely the kind of enculturation of the church I am talking about. In an age of rampant materialism, arrogant nationalism, and preoccupation with self, there is an urgent need for leaders of churches to preach and teach a prophetic word that will disturb all of us, and may save us!

Any serious student of scripture cannot help but be struck by the contrast between the life and ministry of Jesus and the life and ministry of his church. In the face of this reality, there can never be a time when the church can afford to make us feel good all the time, never disturbing or upsetting us. To do so is to compromise the gospel. It is trying to gain the whole world and losing our souls in the process. But any church that takes its prophetic responsibility seriously runs the risk of making people uncomfortable and unhappy to the extent that they may decide not to join or not to stay. This should never be the church's intention. At the same time, it is always a possibility that must not be allowed to influence a church to compromise the integrity of its preaching and teaching and actions.

I am convinced that there is hope for renewed life and vitality in churches that remember their prophetic responsibilities. The call to repentance always holds the promise of new life as God's people turn to the one who is the only true source of their life together. It is in responding to the prophetic word that the church is reborn to new life under the guidance and power of the Holy Spirit. Churches whose members are sometimes uncomfortable are churches that have the greatest potential for significant ministry. A strong church is one whose members recognize that the church does not exist so much to make them comfortable as to lead them into faithfulness. I have no doubt that churches like this will meet the needs of their members, not by simply giving them what they want, but in teaching them how to want the right things.

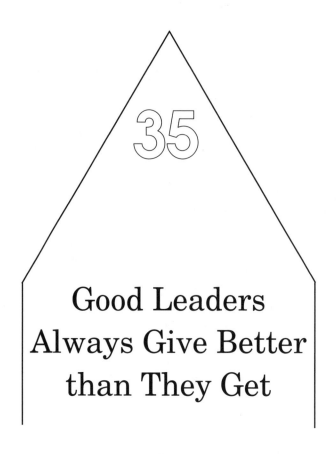

Good Leaders
Always Give Better
than They Get

Rick Atkinson's Book, *The Long Gray Line*, tells the personal stories of several members of the West Point class of 1966. This class had more officers killed in the Vietnam War than any other West Point class. It is a provocative book that provides a distinctive view of the only war this country has ever lost, as seen through the lives of young officers who fought and died in it.

The book begins with a description of the twentieth reunion of the class of '66 as they gathered around the graves of their classmates who are buried in the cemetery at West Point. In remembering their sacrifice for a nation that has become self-indulgent, wondering if their deaths were worth it after all, the West Point chaplain remarked:

"A great leader in any society gives better than he gets. That's just a fact of life."

What a marvelous insight about leadership. Great leaders always give better than they get. This statement is both a description and a challenge. It describes precisely the path effective leaders must travel. At the same time it challenges those of us in leadership or preparing for it to examine ourselves to see if we are willing to give better than we get, precisely because that is what will be required.

The West Point chaplain was, of course, talking about military and political leadership, but his statement applies to church leadership as well. We need church leaders—lay and ordained—who first of all recognize that they will always end up giving better than they get. It's not a matter of giving more than we get. Church leaders receive a great deal when they lead. Despite the struggles and frustrations of church life, ministry gives us so much for which to be thankful. So the issue here is not one of giving more than others give or more than we get in return. It is rather a matter of giving better than we get, which means sacrificing for the sake of others, not in order to be a martyr, but because we know the joy of not counting the cost of being a minister who serves Jesus Christ.

I am aware that there has been much emphasis of late on the need for church leaders to take care of their own needs while serving. This is an important and neglected emphasis. Church leaders, including the ordained, have needs just like everyone else. I tell my students that before they were ever ministers, they were first human beings, and they always will be. They have to remember to care for themselves in the process of caring for others.

Nonetheless, they make a big mistake if they let self-care lead them to think they do not have to give better than they are getting. The price of leadership of any kind, especially in the church, is personal sacrifices. Earlier I discussed the fact that church members seldom get what they pay for from their leaders. They get more. That is because the work to be done requires personal sacrifices:

a shortened vacation, a missed day off, a salary below those in comparable professions. These sacrifices and others like them constitute the reality of church leadership. I do not hesitate to tell my students that if they are not willing to make these sacrifices, then they may as well drop out of seminary right now.

In the church, giving better than you get is what Robert Greenleaf has called "servant leadership." In his book by that title, Greenleaf describes the effective leader as one who leads by serving. He retells a portion of Herman Hesse's *Journey to the East*, which is a story of a band of men on a mythical journey. The central figure is Leo, who journeys with the band of men as the servant who does all their menial chores, and who sustains them with his spirit and his song. Leo is a man of extraordinary presence. All goes well on the journey until he disappears. The group falls into disarray and eventually they abandon the journey altogether. Years later the narrator of the story—one among the band of men—finds Leo again and is taken into the Order that had sponsored the original journey. There he discovers that Leo, the one who had been the servant, is in fact the titular head of the Order, its guiding spirit, a great and noble leader.

Greenleaf draws on this story in pulling together the two concepts—servant and leader—and says that *"the great leader is seen as servant first*, and that simple fact is the key to his [or her] greatness."[1] He goes on to say that those who lead by being servant first do so because that is who they are "deep down inside." Then he says:

> The servant-leader *is* servant first—as Leo was portrayed. It begins with the natural feeling that one wants to serve, to serve *first*. Then the conscious choice brings one to aspire to lead. That person is sharply different from one who is *leader* first, perhaps because of the need to assuage an unusual power drive or to acquire material possessions. For such it will be a later choice to serve—after leadership is established.[2]

The primary difference between the leader-first and the servant-first, says Greenleaf, lies in the fact that the servant-first is focused on the needs of others as the highest priority; that is, that they grow as persons and become healthier, wiser, freer, more autonomous, more likely themselves to become servants.

The servant-leader is a person who is willing to give better than she gets, who is focused on serving rather than on the power of leading. This, I believe, is the attitude of living to which Jesus calls all Christians. We are called to lose ourselves for the sake of the gospel, to bear the cross of burdens for the sake of others. It sounds pious to speak in this way, but it seems to me that servant leadership is the inescapable symbol for the kind of lifestyle Jesus expects of us, especially those of us who lead the church. There is a place for examples, for models of what it means to lead, and an attitude of servant-first seems to me to be the key to the kind of modeling we would want to do.

So much of what we see and hear in advertising and movies and on television reflects our preoccupation with our own needs. The question we were told not long ago by political leaders that we should ask is, "Am I better off than I was four years ago?" It was a question that institutionalized self-centeredness. It is the kind of question a leader who deep inside is servant-first would never ask. The church needs leaders who will be an example of those who are willing to give better than they get. It's what serving in the name of Christ really means. I believe that those who seek to be servant-first leaders will never have to worry about whether or not they are better off than they were four years ago, or a year ago. For they know that to ask such a question is to miss the whole point of what great leadership, especially in the church, is all about.

[1]Robert K. Greenleaf, *Servant Leadership* (Paulist Press, 1977), p. 7.
[2]*Ibid.*, p. 13.

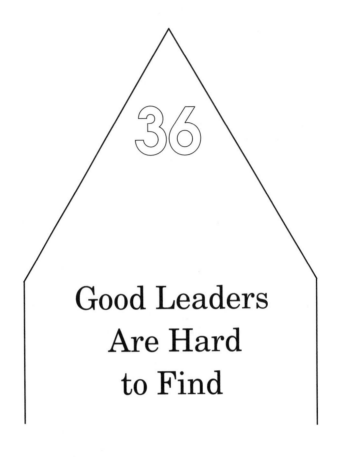

Good Leaders
Are Hard
to Find

One of the most stressful assignments I have is serving on my seminary's admissions committee. All the other members feel the same way. Our task carries the awesome responsibility of making decisions that affect the seminary, the applicants, and the church. Many times the interests of one do not necessarily serve the best interests of the others. At the same time, there is a sense in which we are responsible to God for these decisions, which adds a very different dimension to what we do.

This experience has helped me to see with new eyes the urgent need for the church to nurture and call promising men and women into ministry. The truth is, not all our students have potential for effective leadership in the church. Our situation is no different from other seminaries, as confirmed by a December 1990 article in *Harper's Magazine* on the quality of seminary students today. The study found that the low level of academic ability and extent of emotional/psychological problems made the prospects for leadership in ministry less than promising for many of today's seminarians. In addition, the sense of a traditional call to ministry is missing in more than a few seminary students today. Indeed, at our seminary we have experienced through interviewing prospective students some of them actually becoming offended when we have asked them to tell us about their call to ministry. There was a time when sharing one's sense of call was something a prospective minister wanted to do. Nowadays it is sometimes viewed as an unacceptable invasion of privacy.

One of my colleagues has written a handbook intended to help ministers and church members nurture young men and women into ministry. I believe that God calls people to ministry, but I believe with equal conviction that God has and continues to use the church as a way to do this. I remember the story of the call of the great Baptist preacher, George W. Truett. As a young man Dr. Truett served as the Sunday school superintendent in his home church. This was a lay position of no small importance or influence at the time. Dr. Truett's devotions and leadership were so effective that his friends began urging him to go into the full-time ministry. They saw great potential in him, but he insisted that he had not felt a call from God to be a minister. The congregation's urging and Dr. Truett's resistance went on for some time. Finally some of the church members decided to bring the issue of George Truett's call to ministry to the congregation for a vote. The vote was unanimous—George W. Truett was being called by God to be a minister of the church. Dr. Truett accepted the church's vote as the call of God, and became one of the great preachers and Baptist leaders of this century.

I wonder what happens today to young people like George Truett? Do church members believe that one of their responsibilities is to be used by God to call men and women into ministry? Some probably do, but I am afraid many more do not. My colleague is not finding the kind of interest among clergy or church members in this task that he had hoped he would find. He says the apathy can be discouraging.

There is no greater task nor more important mission for the church than to nurture men and women into ministry. We need the best and the brightest in ministerial leadership. The demands for competency and the will to serve God before anything else are great. The cause of many problems in churches today is poor leadership. At the beginning of the book I spoke about the price churches pay for poor leadership being more than many of them realize. Nothing substitutes for competent ordained leadership. The laity have an important role to play in the church's ministry, but I am convinced beyond any doubt that the best laity in the world cannot make up for poor ordained leadership, which is precisely why church members have a stake in calling the best people they can into ministry.

Ironically, though, many church members do not understand why seminary education is important. They believe that if God calls a person into ministry, that is enough. They need to get on with it. In fact, more than a few of the members of the congregations our students serve believe seminary education "ruins" people for ministry. They think we teach things that either should not be taught or aren't worth being taught because they have nothing to do with "real" life. Just this week I had a student come to talk to me about encountering this kind of attitude in the church where he is serving as a student associate.

What people who think this way do not understand is that good leaders are not simply born. It is true that a person can have natural ability for certain tasks, including ministry. But the making of a minister involves more than skills. It involves the whole person. This means confronting everything about oneself, from abilities and talents to ego and self-centeredness to personal problems and struggles. Sometimes students with much natural ability are less suited for ministry than others who are not so talented simply because of their personality, lack of maturity, inability to cope with issues left over from childhood, or simple intellectual laziness that limits their understanding and vision of church and ministry. Good leaders have to be educated for ministry, just as good doctors and lawyers and teachers have to be educated for what they do.

I am convinced that one of the reasons young people are not attracted to ministry today is because of negative experiences in their home church. Worship is often boring, leaders are resistant to change, ministers do not relate to them very well, members spend much of their time fussing about things that seem unimportant to them. As a result of these experiences, many young people drop out of church when they get old enough to do what they want to do, which nowadays is often mid-teen years. To some extent disenchantment with the church goes with being young. At the same time, though, young people who do not find their home church inviting will hardly be attracted to the ministry as a vocation.

But the search for good leaders need not be confined to the ordained. The same need exists in regard to lay leadership. Churches need the best possible lay leadership they can call forth. This means giving persons leadership positions as a means to get them more involved in the church—a common practice—is an invitation to trouble. More than a few churches suffer from avoidable conflict and experience general decline because of poor lay leadership, leadership that is ill-equipped to lead. The primary responsibility for equipping the laity for leadership lies with the clergy. Thus, the need for good lay leadership comes full circle back to the basic need in the church for good ministerial leadership. Good leaders—lay and clergy—may be hard to find, but the church has a significant role to play in calling and nurturing both. May all of us do our part, for the sake of the church and the world!